OFFICIAL SQA PAST PAPERS WITH ANSWERS

STANDARD GRADE | GENERAL | CREDIT

ACCOUNTING & FINANCE
2007-2011

2007 GENERAL LEVEL – page 3
2007 General Level – 2007 General Level Document Pack
2007 CREDIT LEVEL – page 27
2007 Credit Level – 2007 Credit Level Worksheets
2008 GENERAL LEVEL – page 41
2008 General Level – 2008 General Level Document Pack
2008 CREDIT LEVEL – page 65
2008 Credit Level – 2008 Credit Level Worksheet
2009 GENERAL LEVEL – page 75
2009 General Level – 2009 General Level Document Pack
2009 CREDIT LEVEL – page 101
2009 Credit Level – 2009 Credit Level Worksheet
2010 GENERAL LEVEL – page 113
2010 General Level – 2010 General Level Document Pack
2010 CREDIT LEVEL – page 137
2010 Credit Level – 2010 Credit Level Worksheet
2011 GENERAL LEVEL – page 149
2011 General Level – 2011 General Level Document Pack
2011 CREDIT LEVEL – page 173
2011 Credit Level – 2011 Credit Level Worksheet
ANSWER SECTION – page 185

✕SQA   BrightRED PUBLISHING

Publisher's Note

We are delighted to bring you the 2011 Past Papers and you will see that we have changed the format from previous editions. As part of our environmental awareness strategy, we have attempted to make these new editions as sustainable as possible.

To do this, we have printed on white paper and bound the answer sections into the book. This not only allows us to use significantly less paper but we are also, for the first time, able to source all the materials from sustainable sources.

We hope you like the new editions and by purchasing this product, you are not only supporting an independent Scottish publishing company but you are also, in the International Year of Forests, not contributing to the destruction of the world's forests.

Thank you for your support and please see the following websites for more information to support the above statement –

www.fsc-uk.org

www.loveforests.com

© Scottish Qualifications Authority
All rights reserved. Copying prohibited. No part of this publication may be reproduced, stored in a retrieval system, or transmitted in any form or by any means, electronic, mechanical, photocopying, recording or otherwise.

First exam published in 2007.
Published by Bright Red Publishing Ltd, 6 Stafford Street, Edinburgh EH3 7AU
tel: 0131 220 5804 fax: 0131 220 6710 info@brightredpublishing.co.uk www.brightredpublishing.co.uk

ISBN 978-1-84948-156-4

A CIP Catalogue record for this book is available from the British Library.

Bright Red Publishing is grateful to the copyright holders, as credited on the final page of the Question Section, for permission to use their material. Every effort has been made to trace the copyright holders and to obtain their permission for the use of copyright material. Bright Red Publishing will be happy to receive information allowing us to rectify any error or omission in future editions.

STANDARD GRADE | GENERAL
2007

		KU	HI
	Total		

0010/402

NATIONAL
QUALIFICATIONS
2007

FRIDAY, 25 MAY
10.35 AM – 12.05 PM

ACCOUNTING AND
FINANCE
STANDARD GRADE
General Level

Fill in these boxes and read what is printed below.

Full name of centre

Town

Forename(s)

Surname

Date of birth
Day Month Year   Scottish candidate number   Number of seat

1 Check that a Document pack for use with Question 2(a) has been provided.

2 Answer **all** the questions.

3 Read each question carefully.

4 Write your answers in the spaces provided.

5 Do **not** write in the margins.

6 Calculators may be used.

7 Before leaving the examination room you must give this book to the invigilator. If you do not, you may lose all the marks for this paper.

1. Iago plc returned the following goods that had been bought on credit from Desdemona Dresses.

   2 cotton lycra dresses @ £40 each
   2 leather belts @ £10 each

   Total VAT for the goods is £14·87.

   (a) Complete the Credit Note below, which Desdemona Dresses would send to Iago plc.

CREDIT NOTE

DESDEMONA DRESSES

12 Smith Street
KELSO
TR15 4BY

Telephone: 01573 56423   Email: desdress@htp.co.uk

Credit Note Number: 22

To: Iago plc   VAT Number: 221 13 333
      4 Bonhill Road
      DUMBARTON
      MR3 5PG

Quantity	Description	Unit Price		Cost	
		£	p	£	p
	Less Trade Discount (15%)				
	Net Goods Value				
	Add VAT (17·5%)				
	TOTAL				

Marks: 10

1. (continued)

(b) Name the accounts which would be used to record the transaction from the credit note in the ledger of Desdemona Dresses.

6

(c) Desdemona Dresses is a sole trader and Iago plc is a public limited company. Identify **3** ways a **plc** would differ from a **sole trader**.

6

[Turn over

2. (*a*) Using the **Document Pack provided** make the necessary entries in the ledger accounts of the partnership Calypso Cheeses.

Ledger of Calypso Cheeses

Account Name				Number		1	
Date	Details	Dr		Cr		Balance	
2007		£	p	£	p	£	p

Account Name				Number		2	
Date	Details	Dr		Cr		Balance	
2007		£	p	£	p	£	p

Account Name				Number		3	
Date	Details	Dr		Cr		Balance	
2007		£	p	£	p	£	p

2. (a) (continued)

Account Name				Number	4	
Date	Details	Dr		Cr		Balance
2007		£	p	£	p	£	p

Account Name				Number	5	
Date	Details	Dr		Cr		Balance
2007		£	p	£	p	£	p

(b) Give **2** benefits of preparing a **Partnership Agreement**.

_____

_____

_____

[Turn over

2. **(continued)**

   (c) Explain the meaning of the term **unlimited liability**.

   _____

   _____

   _____

   (d) Explain why a partnership prepares an **Appropriation Account**.

   _____

   _____

[Turn over for Question 3 on *Page eight*

3. The Modern Drama Group provided the following information on 30 April 2007.

Subscriptions	£6,000
Profit on Bar	£3,500
Loss on Plays	£840
New Equipment bought during the year	£2,200
Equipment at start of year	£7,800
Insurance	£120
Hall Rent	£160
Donations received	£500
Honorarium	£200

NOTES
- Hall rent owing at end of year £20
- Insurance prepaid at year end £10
- Subscriptions owing at year end £2,000
- All Equipment is to be depreciated by 10%

(a) From the information provided **select** those items necessary and complete the Income and Expenditure Account on the opposite page.

3. (*a*) (continued)

**Income and Expenditure Account
of Modern Drama Group for the year ended 30 April 2007**

£   £

14

(*b*) Identify **one** item of Capital and Revenue Expenditure from the information provided on *Page eight*.

(i) Capital Expenditure

_____

(ii) Revenue Expenditure

_____

4

[Turn over

3. **(continued)**

   (c) Members' **subscriptions owing** at the end of the financial year would be recorded in the Balance Sheet.

   Tick (✓) the appropriate heading under which this item would appear.

Fixed Assets	
Current Assets	
Current Liabilities	
Long Term Liabilities	

   (d) Explain the following terms when used with **not-for-profit** organisations.

   (i) AGM

   _____

   _____

   (ii) Deficit

   _____

   _____

   (iii) Accumulated Fund

   _____

   _____

   (e) Who would receive an honorarium and why would they receive it?

   Who? _____

   Why? _____

4. (a) Cassio and Emilia are in partnership selling wooden tables.

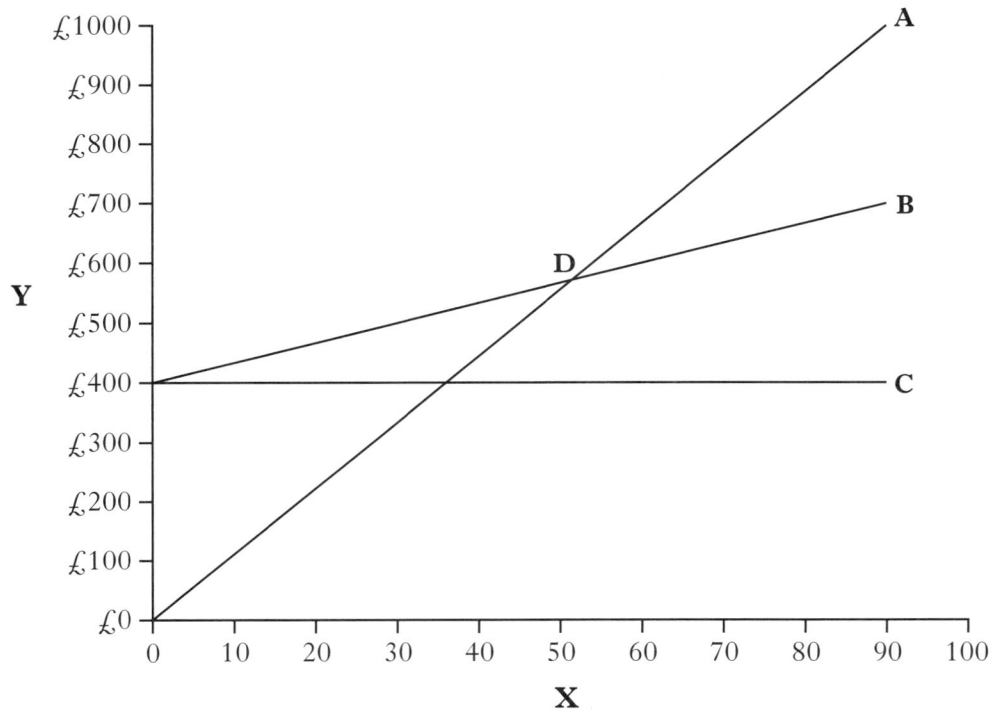

Breakeven Chart for Wooden Tables

Refer to the Breakeven Chart above and complete the table below.

Chart Letter	Chart Name or Label
A	
B	
C	
D	
X	
Y	

4. (continued)

(b) Using the following information complete the table below.

Fixed Costs £200
Variable Costs £1 per unit
Selling Price £2 per unit

Units	Fixed Costs	Variable Costs	Revenue	Profit/Loss
0				
100				
200				
300				

(c) Explain the following terms.

(i) Fixed Costs

_____

_____

(ii) Variable Costs

_____

_____

(iii) Breakeven

_____

_____

[Turn over for Question 5 on *Page fourteen*

5. The following is the Trading and Profit and Loss Account of Ricardo Poseidone a sole trader.

Trading and Profit and Loss Account of Ricardo Poseidone for the year ended 30 April 2007

	£	£
Sales		80,000
less Cost of Goods Sold:		
Opening Stock	10,000	
add Purchases	52,000	
	62,000	
less Closing Stock	6,000	
Cost of Goods Sold		56,000
Gross Profit		24,000
less Expenses		14,000
Net Profit		£10,000

(a) Using the information above, calculate the following.

(i) Average Stock

(ii) Rate of Stock Turnover

(iii) Gross Profit Percentage

(iv) Net Profit Percentage

5. (continued)

(b) Name **2** ratios that could be calculated from the Balance Sheet.

_____

_____

Name of Business	**Zeus**	**Helios**
Rate of Stock Turnover	6 times	9 times
Net Profit Percentage	15%	22%

Using the information above, answer the following.

(c) Which business has been the most successful?

_____

_____

(d) State **one** possible reason why Helios has a higher rate of stock turnover.

_____

_____

(e) Suggest how a firm could improve its Net Profit Percentage.

_____

_____

_____

[Turn over

6. (*a*) Using the information below, complete the following Trial Balance for Telemachas, a partnership, on 30 April 2007.

	£
Capital—Tele	26,050
Capital—Machas	26,050
Drawings—Tele	2,000
Drawings—Machas	1,000
Bank Overdraft	2,400
Debtors	800
Sales	10,000
Sales Returns	500
Purchases	5,600
Rent	100
Creditors	5,000
Discount Received	500
Equipment	60,000

6. (a) (continued)

Trial Balance of Telemachas as at 30 April 2007

	Debit	Credit
Capital—Tele		
Capital—Machas		
Drawings—Tele		
Drawings—Machas		
Bank Overdraft		
Debtors		
Sales		
Sales Returns		
Purchases		
Rent		
Creditors		
Discount Received		
Equipment		
	£	£

Marks: 14

(b) Give **one** reason for preparing the Trial Balance.

_____

_____

Marks: 2

(c) Identify **3** different methods of raising finance for a Partnership.

_____

_____

_____

Marks: 6

[Turn over for Question 6(d) on *Page eighteen*

6. (continued)

(d) Name **or** describe **3** types of errors that would **not** be shown by the Trial Balance.

[END OF QUESTION PAPER]

0010/403

NATIONAL
QUALIFICATIONS
2007

FRIDAY, 25 MAY
10.35 AM – 12.05 PM

ACCOUNTING AND FINANCE
STANDARD GRADE
General Level
Document pack for use with Question 2(a)

Do not return with your examination booklet.

2. (*a*) Use the following documents to complete the ledger accounts for Calypso Cheeses on pages 4 and 5 of your examination booklet.

INVOICE

CALYPSO CHEESES
4 Cave Crescent
ST ABBS
TD2 1RE

No: 4

0191 998768

email: calcheeses@htp.co.uk

Date: 2 May 2007

VAT No: 773 23 49

To: Homer plc
    12 Ancient Avenue
    BERWICK
    TD5 2GH

Quantity	Description	Goods	VAT	Total
10 kg	Mature White Cheddar	£18·00	£3·15	£21·15
5 kg	Creamy Brie	£15·00	£2·62	£17·62
		£33·00	£5·77	£38·77

2. (a) (continued)

CREDIT NOTE

CALYPSO CHEESES
4 Cave Crescent
ST ABBS
TD2 1RE

0191 998768

Date: 9 May 2007

No: 24

email: calcheeses@htp.co.uk

VAT No: 773 23 49

To: Homer plc
12 Ancient Avenue
BERWICK
TD5 2GH

Quantity	Description	Goods	VAT	Total
5 kg	Creamy Brie (damaged)	£15·00	£2·62	£17·62
		£15·00	£2·62	£17·62

Bank of Odysseus 83-15-28
21 Greek Avenue, Edinburgh, EH1 2BY

28 May 2007

Pay Calypso Cheeses
Twenty one pounds 15

A/c Payee

£ 21-15

Georgio Zeus
Homer plc

000002   83-15-28   00127933

[END OF DOCUMENT PACK]

STANDARD GRADE | CREDIT
2007

0010/404

NATIONAL
QUALIFICATIONS
2007

FRIDAY, 25 MAY
1.00 PM – 2.45 PM

ACCOUNTING AND FINANCE
STANDARD GRADE
Credit Level

1 Answer **all** the questions.

2 Read each question carefully.

3 Write your answers in the answer book provided.

4 Candidates should start each question on a new page in the answer book.

5 Calculators may be used.

6 Check that Worksheets for Questions 1(a) and 3(a) have been provided.

Apply VAT where appropriate at 17·5% throughout the paper.

1. On 13 April 2007 Bill Jones sold 4 Wooden Garden Chairs and one Octagonal Garden Table to Gerry Tait on credit.

PRICE LIST 1/1/07 – 31/12/07	
Garden Chairs	
Wood	£25·00 each
Plastic	£15·00 each
Wrought Iron	£20·00 each
Garden Tables	
Square	£35·00 each
Octagonal	£50·00 each
Round	£40·00 each

TERMS
Trade Discount – 10 %
Cash Discount – 5 % one month
VAT – 17·5 %

DELIVERY
£5·00 on orders under £200
FREE on orders over £200

(a) Using the price list above, complete the Invoice (**on the Worksheet provided**) to be sent to Gerry Tait.

(b) Explain **one** benefit to Bill Jones of offering Trade and Cash Discounts.

　(i) Trade Discount

　(ii) Cash Discount

(c) Name **2** accounting documents (other than an Invoice) which could be used in credit transactions and explain their use.

Apply VAT where appropriate at 17·5% throughout the paper.

2. The following account balances appeared on 1 March 2007 in the ledger of Just Jim's, a sole trader.

   Purchases   £2,450
   Sales   £4,500
   Creditor: A Black £600
   Bank   £2,700

   (a) Enter the above balances into the appropriate accounts.

   (b) Record the following transactions in the appropriate accounts.

   02 March   Purchased goods worth £100 plus VAT from K Smith, paying by cheque

   03 March   Returned goods costing £50 plus VAT to A Black

   04 March   The owner took £200 worth of goods for his own use

   05 March   Paid A Black £505 in full settlement of the amount owed

   (c) Just Jim's may have to open a Suspense Account. Explain why this may be required and describe how it would be used.

   (d) The owner of Just Jim's is considering expanding the business. Suggest **and** justify an alternative form of ownership which would assist this expansion.

   (e) Identify **two** disadvantages to the owner of Just Jim's of the alternative form of ownership.

   [Turn over

3. The Bank Statement and Bank Account of Grindles plc are shown below.

Clydeholms Bank plc
15 Greenback Road
Glasgow
G23 5TQ

To: Grindles plc
275 Italian Way
GLASGOW
G21 3RF

Account No 00 299 987

		Dr	Cr	Balance
1/3/07	Balance		1,230	1,230
4/3/07	Deposit		550	1,780
5/3/07	00145	52		1,728
6/3/07	Insurance – SO	120		1,608
7/3/07	00146	220		1,388
9/3/07	Deposit		267	1,655
14/3/07	Cash	100		1,555
16/3/07	Deposit		300	1,855
18/3/07	00147	250		1,605
20/3/07	Cash	100		1,505
21/3/07	Electricity – DD	156		1,349
23/3/07	Deposit		300	1,649
26/3/07	00149	250		1,399
27/3/07	Dividends – BGC		500	1,899
28/3/07	Cash	100		1,799
29/3/07	Bank Charges	60		1,739

3. (continued)

BANK ACCOUNT				
Date	Details	Dr £	Cr £	Balance £
1/3/07	Balance	1,230		1,230
2/3/07	Sales	550		1,780
4/3/07	Travel Expenses		52	1,728
7/3/07	Purchases		220	1,508
9/3/07	Sales	267		1,775
14/3/07	Cash		10	1,765
15/3/07	Furniture		250	1,515
16/3/07	Sales	160		1,675
16/3/07	Sales	140		1,815
20/3/07	Cash		100	1,715
21/3/07	Postages		50	1,665
23/3/07	Sales	300		1,965
24/3/07	Repairs		45	1,920
24/3/07	Purchases		250	1,670
28/3/07	Cash		100	1,570
29/3/07	Sales	450		2,020

*** An error was discovered in the Bank Account on 14/3/07 ***

Using the Worksheet provided you are required to:

(a) (i) update the Bank Account of Grindles plc;

(ii) prepare a statement to reconcile the Updated Bank Account and Bank Statement balances.

(b) State **one** reason why Grindles plc uses a Direct Debit to pay its electricity bill rather than a Standing Order.

(c) State **one** reason why the bank deducted an amount for bank charges.

(d) Grindles plc has issued both Ordinary and Preference Shares. Explain **3** important differences between these types of share.

[Turn over

4. Janet and Jim Anderson are in partnership. Their Current and Capital account balances are given below.

	Current Account	**Capital Account**
Janet Anderson	£2,300 (cr)	£100,000
Jim Anderson	£500 (dr)	£200,000

Their Partnership Agreement states the following.
- Drawings of £500 per month allowed for both partners
- Interest on Capital of 10% per annum on Capital balances
- The first 20% of Net Profit to be transferred to a General Reserve
- Profits/Losses are to be split in relation to Capital balances
- Jim is to receive a partnership salary of £6,000 per annum

During the year to 30 April 2007 both partners took their drawings in full and the partnership recorded a Net Profit of £90,000.

You are required to:

(a) Prepare the Partnership Appropriation Account for the year ended 30 April 2007.

(b) Prepare the Current Account of Jim Anderson on 30 April 2007.

(c) Suggest why the Partnership transfers funds to a General Reserve.

(d) State a reason for Jim Anderson receiving a partnership salary.

(e) Explain why partners usually have separate Current and Capital accounts.

(f) Janet and Jim are considering expanding their business. Identify **2** sources of finance (other than a loan) available to them and give **one** advantage and **one** disadvantage of each source.

5. Ronnie Muir owns a small engineering firm and his Balance Sheet is shown below.

RM ENGINEERING
Balance Sheet as at 30 April 2007

FIXED ASSETS		COST £	PROV FOR DEP £	NBV £
Premises		30,000	0	30,000
Equipment		15,000	5,000	10,000
				40,000
CURRENT ASSETS				
Stock			2,500	
Debtors	4000			
Less: Provision for Bad Debts	400		3,600	
Cash			500	6,600
LESS CURRENT LIABILITIES				
Creditors			1,800	
Bank			400	2,200
WORKING CAPITAL				4,400
				£44,400
FINANCED BY				
Capital at the beginning			40,000	
ADD Net Profit			10,000	50,000
LESS Drawings				5,600
Capital at the end				£44,400

(a) Calculate **2** appropriate ratios to analyse the performance of the business.

(b) Name **2** other ratios which could be used to analyse the final accounts and explain their significance.

(c) Explain **2** reasons why a Provision for Bad Debts is created.

(d) Identify **2** reasons why the "Capital at the end" may be less than the "Capital at the beginning".

6

6

4

4

[*Turn over for Question 6 on Page eight*

6. (a) From the following information, you are required to prepare the Cash Budget of Lucy Liu for the month of **September 2007**.

(1) At the end of August 2007 Lucy Liu estimates a Bank Balance of £13,000.

(2) **SALES**

	July	Aug	Sept	Oct
	£10,000	£12,000	£8,000	£7,000

* Sales are split 50% cash and 50% credit
** Debtors pay on average one month after the month of sale

(3) Lucy Liu will take out a Bank Loan of £12,000 at the beginning of September to help pay for new equipment costing £15,000. This equipment will be paid for in September.

(4) **PURCHASES**

	July	Aug	Sept	Oct
	£8,000	£10,000	£9,000	£6,000

* All purchases are on credit and Lucy Liu takes full advantage of her 2 month credit term

(5) **RENT** — Monthly rent of £200 is paid annually in September

(6) **SALARIES** — Lucy Liu employs 2 workers at an annual salary of £15,000 each—this is paid monthly

(7) **OTHER COSTS** — These amount to £3,000 per month

(b) State **one** benefit to Lucy Liu of preparing a Cash Budget.

(c) Explain why the cash balance might not change by the same amount as the profit made in that month.

(d) Explain the difference between Capital and Revenue Expenditure.

[END OF QUESTION PAPER]

FOR OFFICIAL USE

C

0010/405

NATIONAL
QUALIFICATIONS
2007

FRIDAY, 25 MAY
1.00 PM – 2.45 PM

ACCOUNTING AND FINANCE
STANDARD GRADE
Credit Level
Worksheets for Questions 1(a) and 3(a)

Fill in these boxes and read what is printed below.

Full name of centre

Town

Forename(s)

Surname

Date of birth

Day Month Year | Scottish candidate number | Number of seat

To be inserted inside the front cover of the candidate's answer book and returned with it.

SA 0010/405 6/4370

SCOTTISH QUALIFICATIONS AUTHORITY

Worksheet for Question 1 (*a*)

INVOICE

The Bill Jones Garden Centre

53 Tinto Firs Road
GLASGOW
G15 7YZ

Telephone: 0141 944 4442
Fax: 0141 944 2444

email: bjonesgc@htp.co.uk

Invoice Number: 1225

VAT Number: 1543 236

To: Gerry Tait
245 Coastal Lane
KILMARNOCK
KA1 4RS

Date: 13 April 2007

Terms: 5% one month

Quantity	Description	Unit Price £ p	Cost £ p
	TOTAL		
	Delivery		
	AMOUNT DUE		

Working:

Worksheet for Question 3 (a)

3. (a) (i)

UPDATED BANK ACCOUNT				
Date	Details	Dr £	Cr £	Balance £

(ii) **Bank Reconciliation Statement for the month of March 2007**

[END OF WORKSHEETS]

STANDARD GRADE | GENERAL

2008

0010/402

NATIONAL WEDNESDAY, 28 MAY
QUALIFICATIONS 10.35 AM – 12.05 PM
2008

ACCOUNTING AND FINANCE
STANDARD GRADE
General Level

Fill in these boxes and read what is printed below.

Full name of centre

Town

Forename(s)

Surname

Date of birth
Day Month Year

Scottish candidate number

Number of seat

1 Check that a Document pack for use with Question 2(a) has been provided.

2 Answer **all** the questions.

3 Read each question carefully.

4 Write your answers in the spaces provided.

5 Do **not** write in the margins.

6 Calculators may be used.

7 Before leaving the examination room you must give this book to the invigilator. If you do not, you may lose all the marks for this paper.

1. Elmer Gantry sold the following goods on credit to Sinclair Lewis.

   5 staplers @ £8 each
   2 filing cabinets @ £100 each

   Total VAT for the goods is £33·60.

   (a) Complete the invoice below, which Elmer Gantry would send to Sinclair Lewis.

   ## INVOICE

   No: 426

   Elmer Gantry
   2 Princess Street
   EDINBURGH
   E4 5VR

   Telephone: 0131 45689   Fax: 0131 45692   Email: elmer@coolmail.co.uk

   VAT No: 23245

   To: Sinclair Lewis
        12 Cathedral Street
        GLASGOW
        G28 3BY

   Date: 30 April 2008

Quantity	Details	Unit Price £	p	Cost £	p
	Less 20% Trade Discount				
	Net Goods Value				
	Add VAT @ (17·5%)				
	Total				

10

1. (continued)

(b) Explain why VAT must be included on the invoice.

_____

_____ **2**

(c) (i) Name the accounts used to record the invoice in the ledger of Sinclair Lewis.

_____

_____

_____ **3**

(ii) Name the accounts used to record the invoice in the ledger of Elmer Gantry.

_____

_____

_____ **3**

(d) (i) State **one** benefit to Elmer Gantry of offering trade discount.

_____

_____ **2**

(ii) State **one** benefit to Sinclair Lewis of receiving trade discount.

_____

_____ **2**

(e) Name **one** other type of discount and explain its purpose.

Name _____

Purpose _____

_____

_____ **4**

2. (*a*) (i) Enter the opening Bank Account balance, on 1 April 2008. It is an overdraft of £100·00.

(ii) **Using the Document Pack provided** make the necessary entries in the ledger accounts of Richard Dawkins.

Ledger of Richard Dawkins

Account Name				Number	1
Date	Details	Dr	Cr	Balance	
		£ p	£ p	£ p	

Account Name				Number	2
Date	Details	Dr	Cr	Balance	
		£ p	£ p	£ p	

Account Name				Number	3
Date	Details	Dr	Cr	Balance	
		£ p	£ p	£ p	

2. (a) (continued)

Account Name				Number		4			
Date	Details	Dr		Cr		Balance			
		£	p	£	p	£	p		

Account Name				Number		5			
Date	Details	Dr		Cr		Balance			
		£	p	£	p	£	p		

Account Name				Number		6			
Date	Details	Dr		Cr		Balance			
		£	p	£	p	£	p		

28

2. (continued)

(b) What would Richard Dawkins prepare to check the accuracy of his ledger entries?

_____

(c) Name **3 disadvantages** to Richard Dawkins of being a sole trader.

_____

_____

_____

(d) Explain why Richard Dawkins would prepare the following.

   (i) Trading Account

   _____

   _____

   _____

   (ii) Profit and Loss Account

   _____

   _____

   _____

   (iii) Balance Sheet

   _____

   _____

   _____

[Turn over for Question 3 on *Page eight*

3. The Banmar Reading Group is a not-for-profit organisation.

On 30 April 2008, the closing balances of the Bank Account and Bank Statement were as follows.

Bank Account   £1,800
Bank Statement   £1,725

The following items have been recorded in the Bank Statement but have **not** been recorded in the Bank Account.

Direct Debit – Book Club   £160·00
Standing Order – Hire of Room   £5·00

The following items have been recorded in the Bank Account but have **not** been recorded in the Bank Statement.

Cheques received from members   £300·00
Cheque paid for hire of exhibition hall £310·00
Cheque paid to Amazin Books   £80·00

(a) (i) Update the Bank Account.

Account Name	Bank					Number		1	
Date	Details	Dr		Cr		Balance			
		£	p	£	p	£	p		

3. **(*a*)** **(continued)**

(ii) Complete the Bank Reconciliation Statement.

**Bank Reconciliation Statement
on 30 April 2008**

£ £

3. (continued)

(b) Name **2** duties of the Treasurer of the Banmar Reading Group.

_____

_____

4

(c) The Banmar Reading Group has decided to apply for a council grant.

(i) State **one** reason why this would be better than applying for a loan from the bank.

_____

_____

_____

_____

2

(ii) State **one disadvantage** of applying for a council grant.

_____

_____

2

(d) Name **2** items that could be recorded under expenditure in the Banmar Reading Group's Income and Expenditure Account.

_____

_____

_____

_____

4

4. The following Balance Sheet is that of a sole trader.

**Balance Sheet of W E B Du Bois
as at 30 April 2008**

	£	£
Fixed Assets		80,000
Current Assets	10,000	
Less Current Liabilities	5,000	
Working Capital		5,000
		£85,000
Represented By		
Opening Capital		76,000
Add Net Profit		9,000
		£85,000

(a) Calculate the following ratios.

   (i) **Current (Working Capital) Ratio**

   (ii) **Return on Capital Invested**

4. (continued)

(b) Name **2** ratios that could be prepared from information contained in the Trading and Profit and Loss Accounts.

_____

_____

(c) State **2** characteristics or features of each of the following types of business organisation.

Type of business	Characteristics or Features
Partnership	
Public Limited Company (plc)	
Not-for-Profit organisation (eg club)	

4. (continued)

(d) Explain the meaning of the following.

(i) Capital Expenditure

_____

_____

2

(ii) Drawings

_____

_____

2

(iii) Bad Debts

_____

_____

2

(iv) Counterfoil

_____

_____

2

(v) Debtor

_____

_____

2

[Turn over

5. (a) The table below contains information taken from the business of Gregorian plc.

	2007	2008
Sales	£12,000	D
Cost of Goods Sold	A	£10,000
Gross Profit	£4,000	£2,000
Expenses	B	£5,000
Net Loss	£1,000	E
Current Assets	C	£120,000
Current Liabilities	£60,000	£80,000
Working Capital	£40,000	F

5. (*a*) **(continued)**

Calculate the missing figures (**A** to **F**) in the space below.

All working should be shown clearly.

A _____

_____

B _____

_____

C _____

_____

D _____

_____

E _____

_____

F _____

_____

(*b*) What effect would a Net Loss have on the capital of a business?

_____

_____

(*c*) Explain why using a cheaper supplier could improve the Gross Profit.

_____

_____

(*d*) Why might increasing the selling price **not** result in an improved Gross Profit?

_____

_____

6. The following information was taken from the partnership records of Adeneur & Kohl after the Trading and Profit and Loss Accounts for the year ended 30 April 2008 had been prepared.

	£000	
Capital:		
Adeneur	100	
Kohl	400	
Current Account:		
Adeneur	5	
Kohl	2	Dr
Drawings:		
Adeneur	10	
Salary:		
Adeneur	15	
Kohl	20	
Net profit	85	

NOTE – Profits and losses are to be split evenly between the partners.

(a) From the above information select **only** those figures necessary and prepare the Appropriation Account of Adeneur & Kohl for the year ended 30 April 2008.

Appropriation Account of Adeneur & Kohl for the year ended 30 April 2008

£000s £000s

6. (continued)

(b) Prepare the Current Accounts of Adeneur & Kohl, using the necessary information from part (a) and your Appropriation Account.

Adeneur – Current Account				
Date	Details	Dr	Cr	Balance
		£000's	£000's	£000's

Kohl – Current Account				
Date	Details	Dr	Cr	Balance
		£000's	£000's	£000's

[Turn over for Questions 6(c) and (d) on *Page eighteen*]

6. **(continued)**

   (c) Name the document that partners should draw up before starting the business.

   _____

   _____

   2

   (d) Suggest **2** reasons why a partnership may end.

   _____

   _____

   4

[END OF QUESTION PAPER]

0010/403

NATIONAL
QUALIFICATIONS
2008

WEDNESDAY, 28 MAY
10.35 AM – 12.05 PM

ACCOUNTING AND FINANCE
STANDARD GRADE
General Level
Document pack for use with Question 2(a)

Do not return with your examination booklet.

2. (*a*) Use the following documents to complete the ledger accounts of Richard Dawkins, who owns a pet shop, on pages 4 and 5 of your examination booklet.

INVOICE

Daniel Dennet   No: 4

10 Hartfield Gardens
DUMBARTON
DB2 1TI

01389 99876

Date: 2 April 2008

To: Richard Dawkins
      1 Confidence Court
      OXFORD
      OX2 3GH

VAT No: 17 33 29

Quantity	Description	Goods	VAT	Total
2	Tortoises	£300·00	£52·50	£352·50
5	White Rats	£100·00	£17·50	£117·50
		£400·00	£70·00	£470·00

2. (a) (continued)

		CREDIT NOTE			
Daniel Dennet 10 Hartfield Gardens DUMBARTON DB2 1TI 01389 99876 Date: 12 April 2008 To: Richard Dawkins 1 Confidence Court OXFORD OX2 3GH					No: 1 VAT No: 17 33 29
Quantity	Description		Goods	VAT	Total
1	Tortoise		£150·00	£26·25	£176·25
			£150·00	£26·25	£176·25

Cheque Counterfoil
19 April 2008
Daniel Dennet
(in full settlement)
£273·75
001267

[END OF DOCUMENT PACK]

STANDARD GRADE | CREDIT

2008

0010/404

NATIONAL
QUALIFICATIONS
2008

WEDNESDAY, 28 MAY
1.00 PM – 2.45 PM

ACCOUNTING AND
FINANCE
STANDARD GRADE
Credit Level

1 Answer **all** the questions.

2 Read each question carefully.

3 Write your answers in the answer book provided.

4 Candidates should start each question on a new page in the answer book.

5 Calculators may be used.

6 Check that a Worksheet for Question 1(a) has been provided.

Apply VAT where appropriate at 17·5% throughout the paper.

1. You are employed by New World Computers. One of your duties is to send Statements of Account to customers at the end of the month.

   New World Computers offers the following terms.

VAT	17·5%
Trade Discount	10%
Cash Discount	5% – 1 month

   (a) From the following information, complete the Statement of Account (**on the Worksheet provided**) to be sent to Electronic Retailers on 30 April 2008.

1 April	Electronic Retailers owed New World Computers £300·25
10 April	Sold goods on credit with a catalogue price of £250·00 (excluding VAT) to Electronic Retailers
15 April	Electronic Retailers paid New World Computers £286·15 by cheque in full settlement of the amount owed on 1 April
19 April	Electronic Retailers returned goods valued at £52·48 (including VAT) to New World Computers.

   (b) Name the documents that would have been sent to Electronic Retailers on 10 and 19 April and explain their use.

2. The following information was extracted from the accounts of the Old World Bowling Club.

Assets and Liabilities at 1 May 2007

Premises	£78,000
Bar Stocks	£2,950
Equipment	£12,500
Subscriptions Prepaid	£150
Creditor for Bar Stock	£225
Bank	£1,350

Receipts for year

Bar Sales	£52,334
Subscriptions Received	£10,625
Donations	£750
Competition Entry Fees	£900

Payments for year

Purchase of Equipment	£1,500
Bar Purchases	£25,000
Honorarium	£500
Competition Prizes	£475
Bar Wages	£10,500
Insurance	£600
Greenkeeper's Wages	£6,000
Repairs to Bar	£250

Assets and Liabilities at 30 April 2008

Premises	£78,000
Bar Stocks	£1,890
Equipment	£13,000
Subscriptions Owing	£800
Creditors for Bar Stock	£350
Bar Wages Owing	£200
Bank	£21,384

(a) From the above information, you are required to prepare for the year ended 30 April 2008:

   (i) a Bar Trading Account;
   (ii) an Income and Expenditure Account.

(b) Explain the term "Honorarium" and justify its payment.

(c) The club is considering buying land to create a new bowling green. State **3** sources of finance available to the club, other than a bank loan, and justify your choices.

3. The following Estimated Profit Statement is based on the purchase and sale of 1,000 bicycles by A Murray, a sole trader.

	£	£
Sales		90,000
LESS COST OF SALES		
Purchases		42,000
		48,000
LESS EXPENSES		
Light & Heat	5,000	
Insurance	2,420	
Shop Assistant's Wages	10,080	
Rent	12,500	30,000
PROFIT		£18,000

(a) Calculate the number of bicycles A Murray has to sell to break even.

(b) Calculate how many bicycles A Murray will have to sell to break even if he decides not to employ the shop assistant.

(c) If A Murray does not employ the shop assistant, how many bicycles will he need to sell to make a £36,000 profit?

(d) Explain the difference between a Fixed Cost and a Variable Cost.

(e) A Murray could expand his business by forming a Partnership. State **2** benefits and **2** drawbacks of doing this.

4. The ledger of James Brown included the following balances on 1 May 2008.

Bank Overdraft £350·00
Debtors: A Smith £220·00
G Green £424·00
VAT £110·00 Cr

(a) Open the appropriate ledger accounts and enter the above balances.

(b) Record the following transactions in the appropriate accounts.

2 May G Green purchased goods on credit costing £150 plus VAT

7 May A Smith was declared bankrupt and could only pay £0·25 in the £ of his debt – this amount was received by cheque

10 May £50 of the goods sold to G Green on 2 May were returned as they were damaged

(c) James Brown suffered a number of bad debts over the year. State how he could allow for this in future and what effect this would have on his final accounts.

(d) James Brown records ALL cash transactions in his Cash Account. State an alternative system he could use to record small items of expenditure and describe how this would operate.

[Turn over

5. Utopia plc is a herbal remedy shop. Below are the figures from last year's accounts.

Sales	£100,000
Purchases	£57,000
Opening Stock	£4,000
Closing Stock	£6,000
Expenses	£25,000

(a) Analyse the performance of the business using **3** appropriate ratios.

(b) State **2** ways of improving each of the following.

- Working Capital Ratio (Current Ratio)
- Return on Capital Invested

(c) State **3** benefits to Utopia plc of calculating ratios each year.

(d) Explain **3** differences between Ordinary Shares and Debentures.

6. (a) Name the account which should be opened to allow the final accounts to be prepared when the Trial Balance fails to agree.

(b) Even when the Trial Balance agrees there may still be errors in the ledger accounts. State **2** types of error which are not revealed by the Trial Balance and describe how they may have arisen.

[*END OF QUESTION PAPER*]

FOR OFFICIAL USE

C

0010/405

NATIONAL
QUALIFICATIONS
2008

WEDNESDAY, 28 MAY
1.00 PM – 2.45 PM

ACCOUNTING AND
FINANCE
STANDARD GRADE
Credit Level
Worksheet for Question 1(a)

Fill in these boxes and read what is printed below.

Full name of centre

Town

Forename(s)

Surname

Date of birth

Day Month Year   Scottish candidate number   Number of seat

**To be inserted inside the front cover of the candidate's
answer book and returned with it.**

SA 0010/405 6/4070

Worksheet for Question 1 (a)

NEW WORLD COMPUTERS

43 Inchbank Road
GLASGOW
G15 4FR

Tel: 0141 233 4535   Fax: 0141 233 2332

E-mail: new@freeload.com

STATEMENT OF ACCOUNT

Date: 30 April 2008   VAT No: 245 437 467

Electronic Retailers
22 Silvester Way
CLYDEBANK
CB12 3GL

Date	Details	Dr £	Cr £	Balance £

The last amount in the balance column represents the amount now due ⟶

[END OF WORKSHEET]

STANDARD GRADE | GENERAL
2009

FOR OFFICIAL USE					

OFFICIAL SQA PAST PAPERS 77 GENERAL ACCOUNTING & FINANCE 2009

G

	KU	HI
Total		

0010/402

NATIONAL QUALIFICATIONS 2009

MONDAY, 1 JUNE 10.35 AM – 12.05 PM

ACCOUNTING AND FINANCE
STANDARD GRADE
General Level

Fill in these boxes and read what is printed below.

Full name of centre

Town

Forename(s)

Surname

Date of birth
Day Month Year   Scottish candidate number   Number of seat

1 Check that a Document pack for use with Question 2(a) has been provided.

2 Answer **all** the questions.

3 Read each question carefully.

4 Write your answers in the spaces provided.

5 Do **not** write in the margins.

6 Calculators may be used.

7 Before leaving the examination room you must give this book to the invigilator. If you do not, you may lose all the marks for this paper.

SQA

SA 0010/402 6/3520

1. Deegan & Kerr ordered the following from Grove Office Supplies on 19 February 2009.

   3 operator chairs @ £60·00 each

   1 cross-cut shredder @ £20·00 each

   10% Trade Discount is allowed on all orders

   Total VAT for the goods is £31·50.

   (a) Complete the Order Form below using the above information.

ORDER FORM

Deegan & Kerr
PLUMBING AND HEATING SERVICES
29 Ronan Drive
PERTH
PH3 4GH

To: Grove Office Supplies
90 Strachan Drive
Dundee
DD2 9TT

Tel: 01738 991243
Order No: 256
VAT No: 901 265 771

Date: 19 February 2009

Quantity	Description	Unit Price £ p	Cost £ p
	Less 10% Trade Discount		
	Net Goods Value		
	Add VAT @ (17·5%)		
	Total		

1. (continued)

(b) Name the ledger accounts that Deegan & Kerr would use to record the transaction when the items ordered are received.

_____

_____

_____

6

(c) Grove Office Supplies gives Deegan & Kerr a 10% trade discount.

   (i) What does this mean?

   _____

2

   (ii) Give **one** reason why trade discount is given.

   _____

2

(d) Suggest **2** reasons why Deegan & Kerr may return goods to Grove Office Supplies.

_____

_____

_____

4

(e) State **one** benefit of buyings goods on credit.

_____

2

[Turn over

2. (*a*) **Using the Document Pack provided** make the necessary entries in the ledger accounts of Craigmyle Catering.

Ledger of Craigmyle Catering

Account Name _____				Number ___1___	
Date	Details	Dr	Cr	Balance	
		£ p	£ p	£ p	

Account Name _____				Number ___2___	
Date	Details	Dr	Cr	Balance	
		£ p	£ p	£ p	

Account Name _____				Number ___3___	
Date	Details	Dr	Cr	Balance	
		£ p	£ p	£ p	

2. (*a*) **(continued)**

Account Name _____				Number ___ 4 ___	
Date	Details	Dr	Cr	Balance	
		£ p	£ p	£ p	

Account Name _____				Number ___ 5 ___	
Date	Details	Dr	Cr	Balance	
		£ p	£ p	£ p	

(*b*) Craigmyle Catering will send a Statement of Account to Food 2 U at the end of each month. Explain the purpose of this document.

_____

_____

_____

[Turn over

2. (continued)

(c) Craigmyle Catering operates as a sole trader. Give **2** reasons why the business would benefit from forming a partnership.

_____

_____

4

(d) Both sole traders and partnerships have unlimited liability. Explain this term.

_____

_____

4

[Turn over for Question 3 on *Page eight*

3. (*a*) JS Technologies plc has recently appointed a trainee accountant who produced the company's Trial Balance as at 31 March 2009.

There are **6** entries on the wrong side of the Trial Balance.

You are required to rewrite the Trial Balance, correcting the 6 errors.

JS Technologies plc Trial Balance as at 31 March 2009		
	DR	CR
Wages and Salaries	146,000	
Debtors	44,000	
Purchases		291,000
Bank	27,000	
Debentures	30,000	
Sales Returns	1,500	
Discount Allowed	1,250	
Ordinary Shares	88,000	
Premises	160,000	
Stock		22,750
Discount Received	1,500	
Creditors	30,000	
Sales		534,000
Unappropriated Profit		10,000
	£529,250	£857,750

3. (a) (continued)

JS Technologies plc Trial Balance as at 31 March 2009		
	DR	CR
Wages and Salaries		
Debtors		
Purchases		
Bank		
Debentures		
Sales Returns		
Discount Allowed		
Ordinary Shares		
Premises		
Stock		
Discount Received		
Creditors		
Sales		
Unappropriated Profit		

[Turn over

3. (continued)

(b) Suggest **2** reasons why JS Technologies plc would prepare a Trial Balance at the end of the financial period.

1 _____

_____

2 _____

_____

(c) Even if the Trial Balance totals are equal, there may still be errors in the ledger. Complete the table below with the name of each error. The first one has been completed as an example.

Name of Error
Principle
Reversal
Omission
Compensating
Original entry

Description of Error	Name of Error
A transaction has been completely missed out.	**Omission**
The account which should have been debited is credited and the account which should have been credited is debited.	
The wrong type of account has been used eg Purchases Account instead of Equipment Account.	
The correct accounts were used but the wrong figure entered eg £345 entered instead of £453.	
Two or more errors have cancelled each other out.	

[Turn over for Question 4 on *Page twelve*

4. (*a*) Sophie McPherson owns The Magic Carpet Store which sells carpets, rugs and floor coverings.

From the following information, prepare the Trading and Profit and Loss Accounts for the year ended 30 April 2009.

	£
Purchases	80,200
Insurance	9,600
Sales	124,500
Stock at 1 May 2008	8,000
Rent Received	4,400
Carriage In	1,600
Sales Returns	2,700
Wages	6,400
Furniture (at cost)	25,000
Advertising	5,600
Carriage Out	730

Notes:

(1) Stock at 30 April 2009 was valued at £7,400
(2) Insurance prepaid — £1,600
(3) Furniture to be depreciated by 10% on cost
(4) Wages due — £580

4. (a) (continued)

THE MAGIC CARPET STORE
Trading and Profit and Loss Accounts
for the year ended 30 April 2009

£　　　　£　　　　£

20

4. (continued)

(b) Explain the meaning of the following terms found in a Balance Sheet.

(i) Current Liability

_____

_____

(ii) Drawings

_____

_____

(c) The Magic Carpet Store keeps a Petty Cash Book. Suggest **2** reasons for this.

_____

_____

_____

_____

[Turn over for Question 5 on *Page sixteen*

5. The Treasurer of the Ochil Outdoor Activities Club has provided the following information from the Bar Trading Account for the year ended 31 January 2009.

	£
Cost of Goods Sold	11,250
Opening Stock	1,050
Gross Profit	3,750
Closing Stock	1,200
Bar Sales	15,000

(a) From the information provided, calculate the following ratios.

(i) The Gross Profit Percentage

(ii) The Rate of Stock Turnover

(b) State **2** reasons why the club calculates these ratios.

_____

_____

_____

_____

5. (continued)

(c) Suggest **one** way the club could improve its Gross Profit percentage.

(d) Explain the following terms associated with a not-for-profit organisation.

   (i) Subscriptions

   (ii) Surplus

   (iii) Accumulated Fund

(e) Name **2** items which would appear in a Receipts and Payments Account but not in an Income and Expenditure Account.

(f) Suggest **2** ways in which the Ochil Outdoor Activities Club could raise finance other than by increasing subscriptions.

[Turn over

6. Tynadee plc are producers of golf umbrellas. The estimated costs and revenues are shown below.

Bank Balance at 1 July 2009	£3,800	
Wages	£7,200	per annum paid monthly
Insurance	£200	per month

	June	July	August
Credit Sales	£1,500	£1,820	£740
Cash Purchases	£1,200	£1,100	£1,220

Credit Sales will be paid for in the month following the sale.

Production equipment costing £3,000 will be bought in July and paid in 2 equal instalments in August and September.

(a) Complete the Cash Budget of Tynadee plc for the 2 months ending August 2009.

ESTIMATED CASH BUDGET FOR JULY AND AUGUST 2009

	July £	August £
OPENING BALANCE		
Receipts		
Credit Sales	_____	_____
	_____	_____
Payments		
Purchases		
Wages		
Insurance		
Production Equipment	_____	_____
	_____	_____
CLOSING BALANCE	_____	_____

6. (continued)

(b) Suggest **one** advantage to Tynadee plc of preparing a Cash Budget.

_____

_____ 2

(c) Explain the following terms which relate to a plc.

Debentures _____

_____

Unappropriated Profit_____

_____ 4

(d) Suggest **one** reason why dividends paid to ordinary shareholders of Tynadee plc can vary from one year to another.

_____

_____ 2

(e) Explain the meaning of the following.

  (i) Authorised Capital

  _____

  _____ 2

  (ii) Issued Capital

  _____

  _____ 2

[END OF QUESTION PAPER]

0010/403

NATIONAL
QUALIFICATIONS
2009

MONDAY, 1 JUNE
10.35 AM – 12.05 PM

ACCOUNTING AND
FINANCE
STANDARD GRADE
General Level
Document pack for use with
Question 2(a)

Do not return with your examination booklet.

2. (a)

INVOICE

Craigmyle Catering

Craigmyle Catering
Auchlossan Road
ABOYNE
AB33 1PP

Tel: 013398 80890

To: **Food 2 U**
Unit 10
Ythan Industrial Estate
INVERURIE
AB32 6JN

Invoice No: 3259
VAT No: 221 971 454
Date: 2 March 2009

QUANTITY	DESCRIPTION	UNIT PRICE	COST
		£	£
4	40 cm Serving Platters – Ivory	15·00	60·00
1	3-speed Hand Blender	40·00	40·00
			100·00
	Less 10% Trade Discount		10·00
	Net Goods Value		90·00
	Add VAT @ 17·5%		15·75
	TOTAL		**£105·75**

2. **(a)** (continued)

CREDIT NOTE **Craigmyle Catering**		Craigmyle Catering Auchlossan Road ABOYNE AB33 1PP Tel: 013398 80890	
To: Food 2 U Unit 10 Ythan Industrial Estate INVERURIE AB32 6JN		Credit Note No: 337 VAT No: 221 971 454 Date: 18 March 2009	
QUANTITY	DESCRIPTION	UNIT PRICE	COST
		£	£
1	3-speed Hand Blender (faulty)	40·00	40·00
			40·00
	Less 10% Trade Discount		4·00
	Net Goods Value Add VAT @ 17·5%		36·00 6·30
	TOTAL		**£42·30**

[Turn over

2. (a) (continued)

> **Nicol & Robertson**
> **Solicitors**
> **45 Albyn Street**
> **ABERDEEN**
> **AB11 2SP**

22 March 2009

Craigmyle Catering
Auchlossan Road
ABOYNE
AB33 1PP

Dear Sir

I write to inform you that my client, Food 2 U, has been declared bankrupt today.

As a result, any outstanding debts owed by Food 2 U should now be written off as a Bad Debt.

Yours faithfully

S Robertson

S Robertson
Partner

[END OF DOCUMENT PACK]

STANDARD GRADE | CREDIT
2009

0010/404

NATIONAL
QUALIFICATIONS
2009

MONDAY, 1 JUNE
1.00 PM – 2.45 PM

ACCOUNTING AND
FINANCE
STANDARD GRADE
Credit Level

1 Answer **all** the questions.

2 Read each question carefully.

3 Write your answers in the answer book provided.

4 Candidates should start each question on a new page in the answer book.

5 Calculators may be used.

6 Check that a Worksheet for Question 2(*a*) has been provided.

Apply VAT where appropriate at 17·5% throughout the paper.

1. (a) Use the information below to make the entries in the ledger accounts of the partnership Maxwell and Bell.

   Ledger balances at 1 May 2009:

   Bank Overdraft £1,000
   Equipment £5,500
   M Faraday (Creditor) £ 800

7 May	Bought goods £200 (plus VAT) from Lavoiser on credit
12 May	Purchased equipment from Faraday on credit for £8,000 (plus VAT). A cheque for £2,000 was paid to Faraday with the balance on credit
18 May	Paid for repairs to equipment by cheque for £120 (plus VAT)
22 May	Returned faulty equipment to M Faraday for £80 (plus VAT)

   (b) Explain the meaning of the term **double entry**.

   (c) Maxwell and Bell are considering forming a plc. Justify **one** advantage of the proposed change in relation to each of the points below.

   (i) Capital invested
   (ii) Borrowing
   (iii) Owners' liability

2. (a) From the information below, and **using the Worksheet provided**, complete the Statement of Account which Frege plc would send to Moore Motors at the end of May 2009.

1 May	Moore Motors owed Frege plc £500
7 May	Frege plc sold goods to Moore Motors for £846 (plus VAT). The terms of payment were 5% – 30 days and 10% trade discount was allowed
21 May	Damaged goods were returned by Moore Motors – their debt was reduced by £90
28 May	Moore Motors paid £470 by cheque in full settlement of the balance outstanding on 1 May

(b) Frege plc sells goods on credit. Describe **one** advantage and **one** disadvantage, to Frege plc, of operating this policy.

(c) Name the document used in the transaction on 21 May and state its effect on the Gross Profit of Frege plc.

(d) Explain why a business may need to reconcile the balances on the Bank Statement and Bank Account.

[Turn over

3. Alistair Milestones, a sole trader, discovered his Trial Balance failed to agree. The debit column exceeded the credit by £81. On checking his ledger accounts, he discovered the following errors.

(1) A payment of £92 for rent had been correctly entered in the Bank Account but was entered as £29 in the Rent Account

(2) Discount received for £12 had been entered on the wrong side of the Discount Received Account

(3) An invoice received from B Skinner, a supplier, for £120 (including VAT) had been omitted from B Skinner's account only

(a) (i) Open the required account to make the Trial Balance agree.

(ii) Make the entries in this account **only** to correct the errors.

(b) Explain why the Bank Account can be either a debit or credit entry in the Trial Balance.

(c) Explain why capital expenditure should not be included in the Profit and Loss Account.

(d) Suggest **2** sources of finance, other than a bank loan, Alistair Milestones could use to expand. Outline **one** advantage and **one** disadvantage of each source. (Outline different advantages and disadvantages for each source).

4. Rorty plc provides the following information at 30 April 2009.

	£000
VAT (Dr)	5
Interim Ordinary Share Dividend	1
Bank Overdraft	10
Provision for Depreciation of Vehicles	6
Net Profit	30
5% Debentures	40
Creditors	53
Vehicles	228
Unappropriated Profit on 1 May 2008	9
Issued Share Capital:	
10,000 10% Preference Shares	10
100,000 Ordinary Shares	100
Debenture interest owing	2
Provision for Bad Debts	3
Debtors	22
Electricity paid in advance	4
Expenses owing	2
Stock on 30 April 2009	5

The Board of Directors proposed that:

- the Preference Share dividend is to be paid in full;
- a final Ordinary Share dividend of 2% is to be paid.

(a) Prepare Rorty plc's Appropriation Account and Balance Sheet using the above information.

(b) The Board of Directors of Rorty plc have a policy of retaining profits in the business.

    (i) Explain why the Board of Directors operate this policy.
    (ii) Explain **one** advantage and **one** disadvantage of this policy to the shareholders.

(c) Explain the difference between bad debts and provision for bad debts.

[Turn over

5. The following data is taken from the books of Peter Lyola.

	2008	2009
	£	£
Current Liabilities	5,000	7,000
Closing Capital	106,000	126,000
Fixed Assets	99,000	125,000
Net Profit	26,000	20,000
Current Assets	12,000	8,000
Opening Capital	80,000	106,000

(a) Use the data above to calculate appropriate ratios for the 2 years.

(b) Comment on any variation in the ratios between the years and suggest why the change may have occurred.

(c) Suggest **2** other ratios that might be used to analyse the performance of the business and explain the importance of each.

(d) "When 2 firms are in the same industry, the one with the largest net profit is not necessarily the most successful." Explain this statement.

6. Godel's Trading, Profit and Loss Account for the year ended 30 April 2009 is shown below.

	£
Sales	50,000
Less Cost of Goods Sold	20,000
Gross Profit	30,000
Less Expenses	8,000
Net Profit	22,000

(a) Using the above information, and the notes below, prepare Godel's estimated Trading, Profit and Loss Account for the year ended 30 April 2010.

- It is anticipated that Sales will increase by 10%
- The Gross Profit ratio will be the same as 2009
- £5,000 will be received for renting out property
- Existing expenses will increase by 25%

In addition:

- a bonus of 10% of any sales above £50,000 will be paid to the sales team.
- a bank loan of £2,000 will incur interest of 8% per annum.

(b) Name **one** other financial statement that might be prepared to help the business plan for the future. Explain **2** ways this would assist the business.

Godel is also treasurer of the local badminton club. The only financial record he prepares is in the form of a Receipts and Payments Account.

(c) (i) Explain why this is an unsatisfactory situation.

(ii) Name and justify **2** additional financial statements which may be prepared to present to members at the AGM.

[END OF QUESTION PAPER]

FOR OFFICIAL USE

0010/405

NATIONAL
QUALIFICATIONS
2009

MONDAY, 1 JUNE
1.00 PM – 2.45 PM

ACCOUNTING AND FINANCE
STANDARD GRADE
Credit Level
Worksheet for Question 2(a)

Fill in these boxes and read what is printed below.

Full name of centre

Town

Forename(s)

Surname

Date of birth
Day Month Year

Scottish candidate number

Number of seat

To be inserted inside the front cover of the candidate's answer book and returned with it.

Worksheet for Question 2 (a)

Statement of Account

Frege plc
10 Dalkeith Road
EDINBURGH
E33 5MP

Tel No: 0131 233 567
frege@hotmail.co.uk

Moore Motors
10 Camperdown Avenue
DUNDEE
D22 9PY

VAT No 234 555 231

Date: 31 May 2009

Date	Details	Debit	Credit	Balance
			£

Working:

[END OF WORKSHEET]

STANDARD GRADE | GENERAL

2010

OFFICIAL SQA PAST PAPERS 115 GENERAL ACCOUNTING & FINANCE 2010

FOR OFFICIAL USE

G

	KU	HI
Total		

0010/402

NATIONAL
QUALIFICATIONS
2010

MONDAY, 24 MAY
10.35 AM – 12.05 PM

ACCOUNTING AND
FINANCE
STANDARD GRADE
General Level

Fill in these boxes and read what is printed below.

Full name of centre

Town

Forename(s)

Surname

Date of birth
Day Month Year   Scottish candidate number   Number of seat

1 Check that a Document pack for use with Question 2(a) has been provided.

2 Answer **all** the questions.

3 Read each question carefully.

4 Write your answers in the spaces provided.

5 Do **not** write in the margins.

6 Calculators may be used.

7 Before leaving the examination room you must give this book to the Invigilator. If you do not, you may lose all the marks for this paper.

SQA

SA 0010/402 6/3310

1. McCombie Camping plc returned the following goods which had been bought on credit from Canvas Creations.

   3 Festival Flower tents @ £80·00 each
   1 Camper lamp @ £10·00 each

   10% Trade Discount is allowed on all orders

   Total VAT for the goods is £39·37

   (a) Complete the Credit Note below that Canvas Creations would send to McCombie Camping plc.

CREDIT NOTE No: 559

Canvas Creations
Craigdornan Park
FORFAR
DD8 8CP

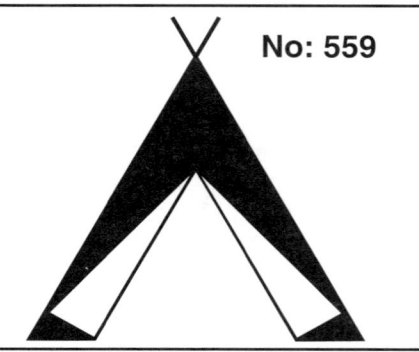

To: McCombie Camping plc
23 St David's Street
EDINBURGH
EH2 2PP

Tel: 01307 55251
Fax: 01307 55252
VAT No: 612 446 091
Date: 6 March 2010

Quantity	Description	Unit Price £ p	Cost £ p
3	Festival Flower tents	80 00	240 00
1	Camper lamp	10 00	10 00
			250 00
	Less 10% Trade Discount		25 00
	Net Goods Value		225 00
	Add VAT @ (17·5%)		39 37
	Total		£ 264 37

Marks: 8

1. (continued)

(b) Name the accounts that would be used to record the credit note details in the ledger of Canvas Creations.

_____

_____

_____

6

(c) Canvas Creations gives McCombie Camping plc Trade Discount. Name another type of discount and explain why it is given.

Name _____

Explanation _____

_____

4

(d) Name the documents which Canvas Creations sends to McCombie Camping plc in the following situations.

	Document Name
McCombie Camping plc buys goods on credit from Canvas Creations.	
Canvas Creations sends McCombie Camping plc a summary of their transactions for the month.	
McCombie Camping plc pays £50 of the amount owed to Canvas Creations in cash.	

6

[Turn over

2. (a) **Using the Document Pack provided** make the necessary entries in the ledger accounts of Gairneybank Garden Centre.

Ledger of Gairneybank Garden Centre

Account Name	Bank			Number		1	
Date	Details	Dr		Cr		Balance	
		£	p	£	p	£	p
14/4/2010	Balance	2,000	00			2,000	00

Account Name				Number		2	
Date	Details	Dr		Cr		Balance	
		£	p	£	p	£	p

Account Name				Number		3	
Date	Details	Dr		Cr		Balance	
		£	p	£	p	£	p

Page four

2. (a) (continued)

Account Name			Number	4	
Date	Details	Dr	Cr	Balance	
		£ p	£ p	£ p	

Account Name			Number	5	
Date	Details	Dr	Cr	Balance	
		£ p	£ p	£ p	

(b) Garden Sundries plc is a Public Limited Company. Explain what the word Limited refers to.

(c) Who owns Garden Sundries plc?

[Turn over

2. **(continued)**

   (d) Name **2** sources of finance, not available to sole traders or partnerships, which Garden Sundries plc could use to expand its business.

   _____

   _____ **4**

   (e) Name the financial statement that Garden Sundries plc could prepare to plan its spending over the next 6 months.

   _____ **2**

[Turn over for Question 3 on *Page eight*

3. The following information has been provided by the Picture Perfect Photography Club.

Assets at 1 January 2009

Cash/Bank	£600	Stock of Refreshments	£500
Equipment	£1,800	Premises	£2,500

Receipts and Payments Account for the year ended 31 December 2009

	£	£
Opening Cash/Bank Balance		600
Receipts		
Members Subscriptions	1,400	
Donations	300	
Grant	800	
Sale of Refreshments	620	3,120
		3,720
Payments		
Purchase of Refreshments	330	
Purchase of Equipment	1,100	
Extension to Premises	750	
Insurance	85	
Cleaner's Wages	165	
Repairs to Premises	90	2,520
Closing Cash/Bank Balance		£1,200

Notes at 31 December 2009

(1) Stock of Refreshments is valued at £320
(2) Cleaner's Wages of £80 are due but unpaid
(3) Insurance has been prepaid by £15
(4) The equipment of the Club is depreciated by 15% per annum

(a) Use the information above to prepare:

(i) a statement clearly showing any profit or loss made on the sale of refreshments for the year ended 31 December 2009;

(ii) the Income and Expenditure Account for the year ended 31 December 2009.

3. (*a*) (i) (continued)

Picture Perfect Photography Club
Statement of Profit/Loss on Sale of Refreshments
for the year ended 31 December 2009

£   £

3. (a) (ii) (continued)

Picture Perfect Photography Club
Income and Expenditure Account
for the year ended 31 December 2009

£   £

3. **(continued)**

   (b) The Club would like to extend its premises again to provide a gallery space to display photographs. Suggest **2** ways it could raise the finance to do this **other than** by a grant or donations.

   _____

   _____ 4

   (c) State **2** reasons why the Club depreciates its equipment.

   _____

   _____ 4

   (d) Explain the following terms which could appear in the Balance Sheet of a not-for-profit organisation.

   Accumulated Fund _____

   _____

   Subscriptions Prepaid _____

   _____ 4

   [Turn over

4. Corrie Cook and Aisha Morrison run Chairs 4U as a partnership. The business produces decorated chairs for children. They have estimated their costs as follows.

Heat and light	£200·00
Decorating each chair	£3·00
Gift wrap per chair	£2·00
Assistant's Wages	£500·00
Shop Rent	£800·00
Cost of chair	£20·00

Chairs 4U is planning to sell the decorated chairs at £40 each.

Corrie and Aisha would like you to calculate the following.

(a) The Contribution that Chairs 4U will receive from the sale of each chair.

Selling Price — Variable Costs = Contribution per Chair

☐ — ☐ = ☐

(b) The number of chairs that need to be sold for Chairs 4U to break even.

$$\frac{\text{Fixed Costs}}{\text{Contribution per chair}} = \text{Break Even Point}$$

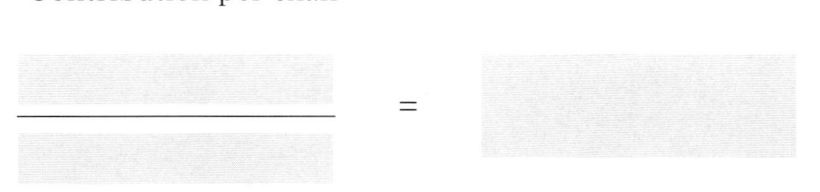

☐ = ☐

(c) The amount of profit Chairs 4U will make if 120 chairs are sold.

$$\left(\begin{array}{c}\text{Total Number} \\ \text{Sold}\end{array} - \begin{array}{c}\text{Break Even} \\ \text{Sales}\end{array}\right) \times \begin{array}{c}\text{Contribution} \\ \text{per Chair}\end{array} = \text{Profit}$$

☐ — ☐ × ☐ = ☐

4. (continued)

(d) When Corrie and Aisha set up their partnership they were advised to draw up a special document. Name this document.

_____

(e) Identify **2** items, relating to the **finance** of the partnership, which might be included in this document.

_____

_____

(f) Before joining Aisha in partnership, Corrie operated a business as a sole trader.

(i) State **2** advantages of being a sole trader.

_____

_____

(ii) State **2** disadvantages of being a sole trader.

_____

_____

[Turn over

5. Peter Canning operates Top Tools, a small business selling work tools to the building trade. He has extracted the following balances from his ledger at 31 January 2010.

Sales	£12,800	Debtors	£580
Wages	£1,900	Purchases	£7,000
Premises	£8,000	Capital	£6,500
Sales Returns	£260	Bank Overdraft	£3,400
Drawings	£3,600	Carriage Out	£360
Rent Received	£220	Opening Stock	£1,220

(a) Use the above figures to prepare Peter Canning's Trial Balance as at 31 January 2010.

Peter Canning
Trial Balance as at 31 January 2010

	Dr £	Cr £
	£	£

5. (continued)

(b) State **2** reasons why Peter Canning prepares a Trial Balance at the end of the financial period.

_____

_____

(c) On checking the accounts, Peter Canning finds the following errors.

(i) No entries had been made in the ledger to record the sale of goods worth £200 on credit.

State how the correction of this error would affect the totals of the Trial Balance.

_____

Give a reason for your answer.

_____

_____

(ii) New Office Equipment costing £400 had been entered into the Purchases Account.

State how the correction of this error would affect the totals of the Trial Balance.

_____

Give a reason for your answer.

_____

_____

[Turn over

6. Alex Ronaldo runs a mobile vehicle repair service. The Balance Sheet for his business is shown below.

Alex Ronaldo
Balance Sheet as at 31 March 2010

	£	£	£
FIXED ASSETS			
Motor Vehicles			19,000
Equipment			5,200
			24,200
CURRENT ASSETS			
Stock		1,500	
Debtors		2,850	
Bank		2,100	
Cash		900	
Prepayment – Advertising		250	
		7,600	
Less CURRENT LIABILITIES			
Creditors	3,200		
Accrual – Wages	130	3,330	4,270
			£28,470
Financed by:			
Capital at 1 April 2009			23,870
Add: Net Profit			4,600
			£28,470

6. (continued)

(a) Use the Balance Sheet on *Page sixteen* to calculate the following ratios for Alex Ronaldo's business.

   (i) Working Capital Ratio

   (ii) Return on Capital Invested

(b) The Net Profit of Alex Ronaldo is shown in the Balance Sheet on *Page sixteen*. In which financial statement is the Net Profit calculated?

_____

(c) State **2** uses of accounting ratios.

_____

_____

6. (continued)

(d) Identify **3** other ratios which Alex Ronaldo might calculate at the end of the financial year.

_____

_____

_____

6

(e) Explain the following terms which may appear in a Balance Sheet.

(i) Bank Overdraft _____

_____

(ii) Drawings _____

_____

4

[*END OF QUESTION PAPER*]

0010/403

NATIONAL QUALIFICATIONS 2010

MONDAY, 24 MAY 10.35 AM – 12.05 PM

ACCOUNTING AND FINANCE
STANDARD GRADE
General Level
Document pack for use with Question 2(a)

Do not return with your examination booklet.

2. (a) Use the following documents to complete the ledger accounts of Gairneybank Garden Centre in your examination booklet.

INVOICE No: 5462

GARDEN SUNDRIES PLC
28–32 Barns Lane
FALKLAND
KY15 7AT

To: Gairneybank Garden Centre Old West Road KINROSS KY13 6YT	Date: 14 April 2010 VAT No: 998 56 31 Terms: Net

Quantity	Description	Goods	VAT	Total
20	50 cm round planters @ £20 each	£400·00	£70·00	£470·00
5	Bamboo wind chimes @ £10 each	£50·00	£8·75	£58·75
		£450·00	£78·75	£528·75

2. (a) (continued)

CREDIT NOTE No: 0241

GARDEN SUNDRIES PLC
28–32 Barns Lane
FALKLAND
KY15 7AT

To: Gairneybank Garden Centre Old West Road KINROSS KY13 6YT	Date: 22 April 2010 VAT No: 998 56 31

Quantity	Description	Goods	VAT	Total
4	50 cm round planters @ £20 each (Damaged)	£80·00	£14·00	£94·00
		£80·00	£14·00	£94·00

Cheque Counterfoil

25 April 2010
GARDEN SUNDRIES
£400·00
Payment on Account
0067543

[END OF DOCUMENT PACK]

STANDARD GRADE | CREDIT
2010

0010/404

NATIONAL
QUALIFICATIONS
2010

MONDAY, 24 MAY
1.00 PM – 2.45 PM

ACCOUNTING AND FINANCE
STANDARD GRADE
Credit Level

1 Answer **all** the questions.

2 Read each question carefully.

3 Write your answers in the answer book provided.

4 Candidates should start each question on a new page in the answer book.

5 Calculators may be used.

6 Check that a Worksheet for Question 1(*a*) has been provided.

Apply VAT where appropriate at 17·5% throughout the paper.

1. Charles Dal is the owner of CD Plumbing Supplies. On 5 April 2010 he sold 3 × 3 m/25 mm Copper Pipe and 2 × Copper Angle Joints to R Greaves who operates as a small plumbing business.

CD Plumbing Supplies PRICE LIST 1/1/10 – 31/12/10	
Copper Piping	
1 metre/25 mm 3 metre/25 mm 5 metre/25 mm	£5·00 each £12·00 each £18·00 each
Angle Joints	
Lead Stainless Steel Copper	£50·00 each £30·00 each £40·00 each
TERMS Trade Discount – 10% Cash Discount – 5% one month VAT – 17·5% **DELIVERY** £5·00 on orders under £200 FREE on orders over £200	

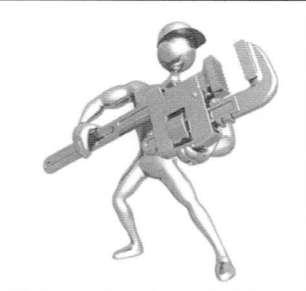

(a) Using the price list above, complete the Invoice (**on the Worksheet provided**) to be sent to R Greaves.

(b) Explain the difference between Trade and Cash Discounts.

(c) R Greaves may have to return some of the items purchased.

  (i) Name the document R Greaves would receive in the event of a return.

  (ii) Explain why R Greaves would not receive a cash refund in the event of a return.

(d) Suggest and justify **2** sources of finance available to Charles Dal for expansion which will allow him to remain a Sole Trader. Give a different justification for each source.

2. The following balances were extracted from the ledger of Kathleen Fitzpatrick on 1 May 2010.

Sales £12,250
Purchases £3,560
Bank £6,220
Machiner £25,600

(a) Enter the above balances into the appropriate accounts.

(b) Record the following transactions, opening new accounts as necessary.

2 May Sent an invoice to Maureen Prescott for £4,000, plus VAT

4 May Sent a Credit Note to Maureen Prescott for £200, plus VAT

7 May Maureen Prescott is declared bankrupt and as a result:
- her solicitor sends a cheque for £500
- a machine with a value of £2,000 is accepted in part payment
- the outstanding amount is to be written off.

(c) Kathleen Fitzpatrick is concerned about the possibility of bad debts.

Explain how the business might decide to deal with any future bad debts and state **2** effects this would have on the final accounts.

(d) When Kathleen Fitzpatrick extracted a Trial Balance from her accounts it failed to balance. Name the account which should be opened and explain how this would operate.

(e) The machinery owned by Kathleen Fitzpatrick may have to be depreciated.

Explain what depreciation is and state **2** reasons why businesses will provide for it.

Marks: 4, 12, 6, 7, 6

[Turn over

3. Gardening Direct plc operates a large gardening centre in Scotland. Its Bank/Cash balance at the end of June 2010 is estimated at £2,500.

It has Issued Share Capital of:

250,000 Ordinary Shares of £1
120,000 5% Preference Shares of £1.

The following estimates have been supplied.

Sales:	May	£31,500	Purchases:	May	£20,000
	June	£37,250		June	£24,300
	July	£42,000		July	£28,780
	August	£34,000		August	£23,000

Rent   £ 2,400 per annum   Insurance   £1,200 per annum
Wages £18,000 per annum   Electricity   £1,200 per annum

NOTES

(1) The directors will pay an interim dividend of 50% of the amount due to Preference Shareholders in July. In August, the Ordinary Shareholders will receive an interim dividend of 2%.

(2) Sales figures include Cash and Credit sales. Cash sales are £5,000 per month. Credit customers will pay one month after the month of sale.

(3) Purchases, which are all on credit, will be paid 2 months after the month of purchase.

(4) All other expenses are paid monthly.

(5) A new Delivery Van will be purchased for £12,000, a deposit of 25% will be paid in July and the remainder will be paid in September.

(a) Using the above estimates and notes, prepare the Cash Budget for July and August 2010. **15**

(b) Explain **2** benefits to Gardening Direct plc of preparing a Cash Budget. **4**

(c) Explain **3** differences between Ordinary and Preference Shares. **6**

(d) Suggest and justify an **alternative** method of financing the purchase of the new van. **3**

4. On 31 May 2010 the Bank Account of the Hi Wave Surfing Club showed a balance of £352·40. On the same date, the balance on the club's Bank Statement showed a Credit balance of £2,962·90.

On checking the Bank Statement against the Bank Account the Treasurer found the following differences.

(1) A Standing Order of £84·50, for rent of the Club's premises, appears only on the Bank Statement.

(2) Subscriptions of £500·00 received by the Club only appears in the Bank Account.

(3) Cheques paid to Surfequip plc for £150·00 and Speed Boatbuilders for £2,500·00 do not appear on the Bank Statement.

(4) A cash withdrawal of £200·00 was correctly recorded in the Bank Statement but entered in the Bank Account as £20·00.

(5) Bank Charges for the month amounted to £25·00.

(6) A donation of £750·00 had been paid directly into the Bank Account by BGC.

(a) (i) Update the Club's Bank Account.

(ii) Prepare a Bank Reconciliation Statement to reconcile the balance in the Bank Statement with the corrected Bank Account balance. **12**

(b) The Hi Wave Surfing Club has used a Standing Order to pay some of its bills. Suggest another banking service it could have used and state how this would operate. **5**

(c) The Treasurer of the Club may receive an honorarium from the Club. Explain the term honorarium. **4**

(d) The Treasurer of the Club has prepared a Receipts and Payments Account and a Cash Budget. Name **2** additional financial statements which should be presented annually at the AGM and explain why they are prepared. **6**

[Turn over

5. The following accounting data was provided by Niven & Brown on 30 April 2010.

Capital account balances 1 April 2009

Niven	£90,000
Brown	£30,000

Current account balances 1 April 2009

Niven	£4,500 dr
Brown	£1,900

Net Profit for the year to 31 March 2010 £23,500

The Partnership Agreement states the following.

- Drawings of £2,500 are to be taken in full by Niven only
- Brown is entitled to a Partnership Salary of £3,500
- Interest on Capital of 10% is to be allowed to partners
- Profits and Losses are shared in proportion to Capital

(a) Using the above information you are required to prepare:

  (i) the Appropriation Account for year ended 31 March 2010;

  (ii) a Current Account for each partner.

(b) State **2** benefits and **2** costs of operating as a Partnership rather than being Sole Traders.

(c) Suggest **one** reason why Brown is the only partner entitled to a Partnership Salary.

6. The following figures have been extracted from the ledger of Brian Boyle Bicycles.

Sales	£120,000
Opening Stock	£6,500
Purchases	£101,000
Closing Stock	£5,500
Gross Profit	£18,000
Expenses	£15,000
Net Profit	£3,000

Figures for the "average firm" in Brian Boyle's line of business are as follows.

- Net Profit %   8%
- Rate of Stock Turnover   15 times

(a) You are required to calculate the **above** ratios for Brian Boyle's business.

(b) State **one** possible reason for the differences between Brian Boyle's business and the "average firm" for **each** ratio calculated. Give a different reason for each one.

(c) Name **2 other** ratios that Brian Boyle could calculate from his final Accounts. Explain his reason for calculating each of these ratios.

[END OF QUESTION PAPER]

OFFICIAL SQA PAST PAPERS 147 CREDIT ACCOUNTING & FINANCE 2010

FOR OFFICIAL USE

C

0010/405

NATIONAL
QUALIFICATIONS
2010

MONDAY, 24 MAY
1.00 PM – 2.45 PM

ACCOUNTING AND
FINANCE
STANDARD GRADE
Credit Level
Worksheet for Question 1(a)

Fill in these boxes and read what is printed below.

Full name of centre

Town

Forename

Surname

Date of birth
Day Month Year   Scottish candidate number   Number of seat

**To be inserted inside the front cover of the candidate's
answer book and returned with it.**

SQA

SA 0010/405 6/3310

Worksheet for Question 1(a)

INVOICE

CD Plumbing Supplies
22 Canal Lane
Knightswood
G17 7TG

Telephone: 0141 959 2197

e-mail: cdplumb@LOL

Invoice Number: 2123

VAT Number: 129 236

To: R Greaves
Golf View
The Village
G15 6RP

Date: 05 April 2010

Terms: 5% one month

Quantity	Description	Unit Price		Cost	
		£	p	£	p

[END OF WORKSHEET]

STANDARD GRADE | GENERAL
2011

FOR OFFICIAL USE

OFFICIAL SQA PAST PAPERS 151 GENERAL ACCOUNTING & FINANCE 2011

G

	KU	HI
Total		

0010/402

NATIONAL QUALIFICATIONS 2011

MONDAY, 30 MAY 10.35 AM – 12.05 PM

ACCOUNTING AND FINANCE
STANDARD GRADE
General Level

Fill in these boxes and read what is printed below.

Full name of centre

Town

Forename(s)

Surname

Date of birth
Day Month Year   Scottish candidate number   Number of seat

1 Check that a Document pack for use with Question 2(a) has been provided.

2 Answer **all** the questions.

3 Read each question carefully.

4 Write your answers in the spaces provided.

5 Do **not** write in the margins.

6 Calculators may be used.

7 Before leaving the examination room you must give this book to the Invigilator. If you do not, you may lose all the marks for this paper.

SQA

SA 0010/402 6/2910

1. Sam Stenhouse runs a pottery business. On 26 April 2011 he sold the following items to Middleton plc on credit.

    10 pasta bowls @ £8·00 each
    4 large platters @ £10·00 each

    5% Trade Discount is allowed on all orders

    Total VAT for the goods is £19·95

    (a) Complete the invoice below that Sam Stenhouse would send to Middleton plc.

    INVOICE   No: 3354

    SAM STENHOUSE
    92 Mainsacre Road
    NAIRN
    IV12 8YY

    To: Middleton plc
    48–52 Ythan Street
    ELLON
    AB41 4BB

    Tel: 01358 702225
    VAT No: 8276 0067
    Date: 28 April 2011

Quantity	Description	Unit Price		Cost	
		£	p	£	p
	Less 5% Trade Discount				
	Net Goods Value				
	Add VAT @ 17·5%				
	Total			£	

1. **(continued)**

   (b) Name the accounts that would be used to record the invoice details in the ledger of Middleton plc.

   _____

   _____

   _____   6

   (c) Sam Stenhouse gives Middleton plc a trade discount of 5%. Give **2** reasons why trade discount is given.

   _____

   _____   4

   (d) (i) Name the document which Sam Stenhouse would send to Middleton plc at the end of the month.

   _____   2

   (ii) Explain why Sam Stenhouse would send this document.

   _____

   _____   2

   (e) State **one** benefit to Middleton plc of buying goods on credit from Sam Stenhouse.

   _____

   _____   2

[Turn over

2. (a) (i) In the ledger of Wholesale DIY, enter the balance of £350 owed by debtor, Castle Contractors, on 1 February 2011.

   (ii) **Using the Document Pack provided** make the necessary entries in the ledger accounts of Wholesale DIY.

Ledger of Wholesale DIY

Account Name _____ Number ___1___

Date	Details	Dr £	p	Cr £	p	Balance £	p

Account Name _____ Number ___2___

Date	Details	Dr £	p	Cr £	p	Balance £	p

Account Name _____ Number ___3___

Date	Details	Dr £	p	Cr £	p	Balance £	p

2. (a) (ii) (continued)

Account Name		Number		4	
Date	Details	Dr	Cr	Balance	
		£ p	£ p	£ p	

Account Name		Number		5	
Date	Details	Dr	Cr	Balance	
		£ p	£ p	£ p	

Account Name		Number		6	
Date	Details	Dr	Cr	Balance	
		£ p	£ p	£ p	

20

2. (continued)

(b) Once the double entry in the ledger of Wholesale DIY is complete, it is important to check the accuracy of the entries before preparing the final accounts.

(i) Explain the meaning of **double entry**.

_____

_____ 2

(ii) State what Wholesale DIY would prepare to **check the accuracy** of the double entry.

_____ 2

(iii) Wholesale DIY is operated by Ritchie Paterson, a sole trader. Name the **final accounts** that Wholesale DIY would prepare.

_____

_____ 4

(c) Ritchie Paterson of Wholesale DIY is considering going into partnership with his friend, Bryan Richmond.

(i) State **2 advantages** of forming a partnership.

_____

_____

_____

_____ 4

(ii) State **2 disadvantages** of forming a partnership.

_____

_____

_____

_____ 4

[Turn over for Question 3 on *Page eight*

3. (a) GoodBrand Media plc have forecast the following costs and revenues. Use this information to complete the Cash Budget below.

Bank balance at 1 July 2011   £4,000
Rent   £1,200 per month
Wages   £9,000 per annum paid monthly
Advertising   £400 per month

	June	July	August
Credit Sales	£1,800	£2,400	£1,500
Cash Sales	£1,100	£1,200	£1,500
Cash Purchases	£1,500	£1,300	£1,250

- Credit Sales are paid for in the month following sale
- ICT equipment costing £5,250 is to be purchased in July. It will be paid for in 3 equal instalments over the period August to October

Cash Budget for July and August 2011

	July £	August £
Opening Balance		
Receipts		
Credit Sales		
Cash Sales		
Payments		
Purchases		
Rent		
Wages		
Advertising		
ICT Equipment		
Closing Balance		

16

3. **(continued)**

   (b) From the descriptions given in the table below, identify the **3** sources of finance which are available to a public limited company.

Description	Source of Finance
Borrowing specifically for the purchase of property	
Long-term loans which must be repaid in full at an agreed date	
Short-term borrowing to ease cash flow	

   (c) Explain the following terms which may appear in the final accounts of GoodBrand Media plc.

   (i) Dividend _____

   _____

   (ii) Wages Accrued _____

   _____

   (d) The shareholders of GoodBrand Media plc have limited liability. Explain the term "limited liability".

   _____

   _____

[Turn over

4. The following Bank Statement was received by Larkside Drama Club for the month of April 2011.

NORTH LINK BANK plc
44 Augustus Road
Inverness
IV2 8HJ

Larkside Drama Club
Castle Hall
Inverness
IV2 2PQ

Account No: 00576254
Branch Code: 20-66-78
Date: 30 April 2011

Date	Description	Dr £	Cr £	Balance £
1 April	Balance			150·00 DR
9 April	025514	30·00		180·00 DR
11 April	Deposit		550·00	370·00 CR
12 April	DD – Topdeal Insurance	✗ 35·00		335·00 CR
19 April	025515	50·00		285·00 CR
24 April	BGC – Sponsorship		✗ 44·50	329·50 CR
28 April	Bank Charges	✗ 14·50		315·00 CR

The Club's Bank Account for the month of April is shown below.

BANK ACCOUNT

Date	Details	Dr £	Cr £	Balance £
1 April	Balance			150·00 CR
4 April	Refreshments		30·00	180·00 CR
8 April	Subscriptions	550·00		370·00 DR
12 April	Fabulous Fabrics		50·00	320·00 DR
18 April	Jack Joinery Ltd		✗ 75·00	245·00 DR
23 April	Advertising		✗ 20·00	225·00 DR
29 April	Donation	✗ 120·00		345·00 DR

The differences between the 2 documents have been marked with a cross (✗)

4. **(continued)**

    (a) Update the Bank Account of Larkside Drama Club on 30 April 2011.

BANK ACCOUNT				
Date	Details	Dr £	Cr £	Balance £

    5

    (b) Complete the Bank Reconciliation Statement below for the month of April, to reconcile the Bank Statement Balance with the updated Bank Account balance.

**Bank Reconciliation Statement
of Larkside Drama Club as at 30 April 2011**

6

4. **(continued)**

   (c) Bank Charges are included in the Club's Bank Statement. Give **one** reason why a bank charges its customers.

   _____

   _____ 2

   (d) Identify the job title of the member of Larkside Drama Club who would be responsible for preparing the Bank Reconciliation Statement.

   _____ 2

   (e) Explain the following terms which relate to not-for-profit organisations.

   Deficit _____

   _____

   AGM _____

   _____

   Honorarium _____

   _____

   Subscriptions _____

   _____ 8

[Turn over for Question 5 on *Page fourteen*

5. The following financial information has been provided by Steve Samir, a fashion retailer.

Trading and Profit and Loss Account of Steve Samir for the year ended 31 March 2011

	£	£
Sales		120,000
less Cost of Goods Sold		
Opening Stock	15,000	
add Purchases	58,000	
Carriage In	8,000	
	81,000	
less Closing Stock	9,000	
Cost of Goods Sold		72,000
Gross Profit		48,000
less Expenses		33,000
Net Profit		£15,000

(a) Using the information above, calculate the following.

   (i) Rate of Stock Turnover

   (ii) Gross Profit Percentage

   (iii) Net Profit Percentage

5. (continued)

(b) Explain the term "Carriage In" which appears in Steve Samir's Trading Account.

_____

_____

2

(c) The Rate of Stock Turnover for a similar business to Steve Samir's has increased from 10 times to 12 times. Suggest **one** reason for this change.

_____

_____

2

(d) Name **2** other ratios that Steve Samir may decide to calculate.

_____

_____

4

(e) Steve Samir's business shows a Net Profit on 31 March 2011. Explain the effect of Net Profit on the capital of the business.

_____

_____

2

[Turn over

6. (a) Ruben Benito and Charles Moreno are in partnership running a restaurant business.

The following information was taken from the financial records of the partnership on 30 April 2011.

		£
Capital	Benito	150,000
	Moreno	200,000
Salary	Benito	8,000
	Moreno	10,000
Current Account	Benito	3,000
	Moreno	1,000
Drawings	Moreno	5,000
Net Profit		42,000

NOTE: Profits and losses are to be shared between Benito and Moreno in the ratio 2:1

From the information provided above, select the necessary figures and prepare the Appropriation Account of Benito and Moreno for the year ended 30 April 2011.

Appropriation Account of Benito and Moreno for the year ended 30 April 2011

£ £

8

6. (continued)

(b) Prepare the Current Account of Moreno using the relevant information from part (a) and the Appropriation Account you have just prepared.

Moreno – Current Account				
Date	Details	Dr £	Cr £	Balance £

4

(c) (i) Explain the term Capital Expenditure.

_____

_____

2

(ii) Give **one** example of Capital Expenditure.

_____

2

(iii) Explain the term Revenue Expenditure.

_____

_____

2

(iv) Give **one** example of Revenue Expenditure.

_____

2

[Turn over for Question 6(d) on *Page eighteen*

6. (continued)

(d) Explain the following terms which could appear in the final accounts of a business.

Depreciation _____

_____ 2

Bad Debts _____

_____ 2

Creditor _____

_____ 2

[END OF QUESTION PAPER]

0010/403

NATIONAL
QUALIFICATIONS
2011

MONDAY, 30 MAY
10.35 AM – 12.05 PM

ACCOUNTING AND
FINANCE
STANDARD GRADE
General Level
Document pack for use with
Question 2(a)

Do not return with your examination booklet.

2. (a) Use the following documents to complete the ledger accounts of Wholesale DIY in your examination booklet.

WHOLESALE DIY
Bellside Industrial Estate
STONEHAVEN
AB39 3DD

Tel: 01569 262076

To: Castle Contractors
 48 Duffus Road
 Elgin
 IV30 4ND

Invoice No: 9947

VAT No: 414 773 008

Date: 5 February 2011

Quantity	Description	Goods	VAT	Total
		£	£	£
10 packs	Light Oak Flooring @ £36 per pack	360·00	59·98	419·98
5 boxes	Riva Floor Tiles @ £18 per box	90·00	14·96	104·96
	Terms: 5% monthly	450·00	74·94	524·94

COPY

2. (a) (continued)

WHOLESALE DIY Bellside Industrial Estate STONEHAVEN AB39 3DD Tel: 01569 262076			CREDIT NOTE		
To: Castle Contractors 48 Duffus Road Elgin IV30 4ND			Credit Note No: 301 VAT No: 414 773 008 Date: 14 February 2011		
Quantity	Description		Goods	VAT	Total
			£	£	£
2 packs	Light Oak Flooring @ £36 per pack		72·00	11·97	83·97
			72·00	11·97	83·97

[Turn over

2. (a) (continued)

Castle Contractors
48 Duffus Road
Elgin
IV30 4ND

RM/LP

18th February 2011

Wholesale DIY
Bellside Industrial Estate
STONEHAVEN
AB39 3DD

Dear Sir

I attach below our cheque for £327·50 in full settlement of the amount owed to you on 1 February 2011.

Yours faithfully

Ross Morgan

Ross Morgan
Accountant

CAIRD BANK plc 29-12-62
82 Hightown Road, DUNDEE, DD2 6HI

Pay *Wholesale DIY* Date *18th Feb 2011*

Three Hundred and Twenty Seven Pounds 50 pence £327.50

CASTLE CONTRACTORS

Jackie Castle

007419 29-12-62 72566013

[END OF DOCUMENT PACK]

STANDARD GRADE | CREDIT

2011

0010/404

NATIONAL
QUALIFICATIONS
2011

MONDAY, 30 MAY
1.00 PM – 2.45 PM

ACCOUNTING AND
FINANCE
STANDARD GRADE
Credit Level

1 Answer **all** the questions.

2 Read each question carefully.

3 Write your answers in the answer book provided.

4 Candidates should start each question on a new page in the answer book.

5 Calculators may be used.

6 Check that a Worksheet for Question 1(a) has been provided.

Apply VAT where appropriate at 17·5% throughout the paper.

1. Robert & Tommy Rose are in a partnership which specialises in golf equipment. Credit customers are offered the following terms.

Trade Discount	10%
VAT	17·5%
Cash Discount	5% one month

   On 31 March 2011 a Statement of Account is sent to Terry Woods containing the following details.

1 March	Balance due £524·81
7 March	Terry Woods bought equipment costing £780·00 (**before** the above terms were applied)
10 March	Terry Woods paid Robert & Tommy Rose £502·31 by cheque in full settlement of the balance outstanding on 1 March
15 March	Terry Woods returned some of the equipment purchased on 7 March as it was faulty. The value of the goods (**after** the above terms were applied) was £265·00

   (a) Complete the Statement of Account (**on the Worksheet provided**) to be sent to Terry Woods on 31 March. **9**

   (b) Suggest a reason why Robert & Tommy Rose offer Cash Discount to their customers. **2**

   (c) Name the document which would have been sent by Robert & Tommy Rose on 15 March and explain its use. **3**

   (d) Robert & Tommy Rose are considering becoming a plc.

   Suggest **2** advantages and **2** disadvantages of this to the partners. **8**

2. Maggie MacIntyre operates a small business buying and selling beauty products. The following balances were taken from her ledger on 1 March 2011.

   Cash   £455·00
   Bank Overdraft £220·00
   Equipment   £2,100·00

   (a) Open the accounts with the above balances.

   (b) Record the following transactions in the ledger.

2 March	Paid by cheque for 4 desktop fans for office use. Fans cost £30·00 each plus VAT
4 March	Maggie decided to take one of the fans purchased on 2 March for her own use at home
6 March	Cash sales £200·00 plus VAT
8 March	One of the fans bought on 2 March was returned as it was faulty. A cash refund was received
10 March	Maggie kept £50·00 cash in the till and transferred the rest to the bank

   (c) At the moment, Maggie operates her business on a strictly "cash only" basis ie all customers pay at the time of sale. Suggest **2** benefits and **2** costs of operating on a credit basis.

   (d) Maggie is also a member of her local Tennis Club. The club only provides its members with a Receipts and Payments Account. Maggie has complained that this does not provide enough information. Suggest **2** other Financial Statements which could be provided and explain their significance.

[Turn over

3. JMac plc make and sell hamburgers for the catering trade. The following Profit Statement relates to last month when 30,000 hamburgers were made and sold.

Profit Statement

	£	£
Sales		15,000
Less Cost of sales		9,000
		6,000
Less Expenses		
Rent	2,000	
Insurance	200	
Wages	1,800	4,000
Profit		2,000

(a) Calculate how many hamburgers JMac plc must sell to break even. — 7

(b) Wages are expected to increase to £2,000 next month. Calculate how many hamburgers JMac plc will have to sell to break even. — 4

(c) If the wages rise, as expected, calculate how many hamburgers JMac plc will have to sell to make a profit of £5,000. — 4

(d) State the effect each of the following will have on the break-even-point and explain why.

   (i) Selling price increases while all costs remain the same.

   (ii) Cost of sales decreases while all other costs and selling price remain constant. — 6

(e) (i) Suggest **2** sources of finance, **that are only available to a plc**, which would allow JMac plc to expand.

   (ii) Give **one** advantage and **one** disadvantage of each source suggested. **(Advantages/disadvantages of each source must be different.)** — 10

4. Malcolm Docherty operates a small fishing supplies business called "Flies Are Us". The following information was extracted from his ledger on 30 April 2011.

	£
Purchases	24,650
Debtors	3,000
Loan	2,000
Wages	20,000
Drawings	1,500
Stock – 1 May 2010	4,600
Carriage Out	350
Carriage In	175
Sales	73,250
Returns Out	900
Electricity	1,540
Provision for Depreciation of Van	3,000
Van (at cost)	10,000
Bad Debts	150
Rent Received	1,200
Provision for Bad Debts	200
Creditors	2,500
Loan Interest	200

NOTES

- Stock value at 30 April 2011 £5,000
- Electricity prepaid £90
- Wages accrued £1,000
- Provide for depreciation of the van at 15% on cost
- The provision for bad debts is to be adjusted to 10% of Debtors

(a) Select the necessary information and prepare the Trading, Profit and Loss Accounts for the year.

(b) Explain the difference between the following terms.

    (i) Carriage In and Carriage Out

    (ii) Debtors and Creditors

    (iii) Bad Debts and Provision for Bad Debts

Marks: 23, 12

[Turn over

5. Brian and Pat Boyle run a corner shop. The total of the Dr column in the Trial Balance was £89,260 and the total of the Cr column was £90,152.

(a) Open the necessary account which will allow the Trial Balance to balance.

On checking the entries it was discovered that the following errors had been made.

- Sales Returns of £250 had been correctly entered in the Debtor and VAT Accounts, but had been recorded on the wrong side of the Sales Returns Account.
- Although recorded in the Bank Account, there was no other record made of £466 withdrawn by the owner Brian Boyle.
- Cash Sales of £240 were correctly entered in the Sales and VAT Accounts but recorded as £24 in the Cash Account.
- The Purchases Account was over-added by £290.

(b) Correct these errors showing **only** the necessary entries to be made in the account opened in part (a) above.

The following errors were discovered **after** the corrections above were made.

- Payment of £45 for the purchase of petrol for the Delivery Van was correctly entered in the Bank Account, but mistakenly entered in the Delivery Vans Account.
- Purchases of £157 on credit from Jack Green had been recorded in the account Jim Green.

(c) State the name given to each of the above types of error.

(d) Describe **2** other types of error which would not have been detected by the Trial Balance.

(e) Explain why the above errors would not have been detected by the Trial Balance.

6. The following information was extracted from the Balance Sheets of 2 firms in the same line of business.

	Peddlars	**Cycling World**
Fixed Assets	£100,000	£40,000
Current Assets	£11,000	£4,500
Current Liabilities	£7,750	£1,500
Working Capital	£3,250	£3,000
	£103,250	£43,000
Financed by		
Opening Capital	£85,000	£30,000
Net Profit	£35,000	£25,000
	£120,000	£55,000
Drawings	£16,750	£12,000
Closing Capital	£103,250	£43,000

(a) Calculate appropriate ratios for both firms. **8**

(b) Name and explain the possible use of **2** other accounting ratios.
   (Give a different use for each ratio named.) **6**

(c) Identify the type of business organisation of the 2 firms above. Give a reason to support your answer. **3**

(d) State **2** reasons why "Closing Capital" may be less than "Opening Capital". **4**

(e) Suggest **2** banking services a business could use to pay an electricity bill and justify the most appropriate service. **4**

[END OF QUESTION PAPER]

FOR OFFICIAL USE

C

0010/405

NATIONAL
QUALIFICATIONS
2011

MONDAY, 30 MAY
1.00 PM – 2.45 PM

ACCOUNTING AND
FINANCE
STANDARD GRADE
Credit Level
Worksheet for Question 1(a)

Fill in these boxes and read what is printed below.

Full name of centre

Town

Forename

Surname

Date of birth
Day Month Year   Scottish candidate number   Number of seat

**To be inserted inside the front cover of the candidate's
answer book and returned with it.**

SQA

SA 0010/405 6/2810

Worksheet for Question 1(a)

ROBERT & TOMMY ROSE

18 Fairview Road
GLASGOW
G19 4FR

Telephone: 0141–423–1212   Fax: 0141–423–2112
e-mail: old@linkscourse.com

STATEMENT OF ACCOUNT

Date: 31 March 2011   VAT Number: 135 787 337

Terry Woods
"The Bunker"
AYR
ST1 1AR

Date	Details	Dr £	Cr £	Balance £

The last amount in the balance column represents the amount now due ⎯⎯⎯↑

[END OF WORKSHEET]

STANDARD GRADE | ANSWER SECTION

BrightRED ANSWER SECTION FOR

SQA STANDARD GRADE
GENERAL AND CREDIT
ACCOUNTING & FINANCE 2007–2011

ACCOUNTING & FINANCE GENERAL 2007

1. (a)

Credit Note

Desdemona Dresses

12 Smith Street
KELSO
TR15 4BY

Telephone: 01573 56423   Email: desdress@htp.co.uk

Credit Note Number: 22   VAT Number: 221 13 333

To: Iago plc
4 Bonhill Road
DUMBARTON
MR3 5PG

Quantity	Description	Unit Price		Cost	
		£	p	£	p
2	Cotton Lycra Dresses	40	00	80	00
2	Leather Belts	10	00	20	00
				100	00
	Less Trade Discount (15%)			15	00
	Net Goods Value			85	00
	Add VAT (17·5%)			14	87
	TOTAL			£99	87

(b) • Sales Returns
  • VAT
  • Iago plc

(c) *Any three from:*
  • Plc has shareholders
  • Capital raised by issuing shares
  • Number of owners are unlimited
  • Capital much greater
  • Must publish accounts
  • Can issue debentures
  • Dividends are paid
  • Limited liability
  • Run by Board of Directors
  • Many legal requirements
  • Must hold an AGM
  • Shares sold on the stock exchange
  • Plc has an Appropriation Account
  • Plc issues shares to shareholders
  • Profit is shared among shareholders
  • Greater borrowing power

2. (a) Ledger of Calypso Cheeses

Account Name	Sales				Number 1	
Date	Details	Dr		Cr	Balance	
2007		£	p	£	p	£	p
2 May	Homer plc			33	00	33	00

Account Name	VAT				Number 2	
Date	Details	Dr		Cr	Balance	
2007		£	p	£	p	£	p
2 May	Homer plc			5	77	5	77
15 May	Homer plc	2	62			3	15

Account Name	Homer plc				Number 3	
Date	Details	Dr		Cr	Balance	
2007		£	p	£	p	£	p
2 May	Sales & VAT	38	77			38	77
9 May	Sales Returns & VAT			17	62	21	15
28 May	Bank			21	15	0	00

Account Name	Sales Returns				Number 4	
Date	Details	Dr		Cr	Balance	
2007		£	p	£	p	£	p
9 May	Homer plc	15	00			15	00

Account Name	Bank				Number 4	
Date	Details	Dr		Cr	Balance	
2007		£	p	£	p	£	p
28 May	Homer plc	21	15			21	15

(b) *Any two from:*
  • States capital (money) invested by each partner
  • Fewer disagreements
  • States amount of salary paid to partners
  • What happens if a partner dies, retires or leaves
  • What happens if a new partner joins
  • States interest on capital and drawings
  • States limitations on drawings
  • States how profit/losses are shared
  • Legally binding on partners. It could be used in court.
  • May state duties/rights/responsibilities of partners
  • States how much of the business you own

(c) In the event of the business going bankrupt the owner may have to pay debts from personal assets

(d) *Any one from:*
  • To record the sharing out of the net profit/loss
  • To record partnership salaries, interest on capital, interest on drawings and transfer to general reserve.
  • Money shared out.

3. (a) Income and Expenditure Account of Modern Group for the year ended 30 April 2007

INCOME   £   £
Subscriptions [6,000 + 2,000]   8,000
Bar Profit   3,500
Donations   500

                                                  12,000

EXPENDITURE
Loss on Plays   840
Depreciation (10,000 × 10%)   1,000
Insurance (120 − 10)   110
Hall Rent (160 + 20)   180
Honorarium   200
                                                   2,330
Surplus   £9,670

(b) (i) Capital Expenditure: Equipment (new or old)
    (ii) Revenue Expenditure *(any one from)*:
        • Insurance
        • Rent
        • Honorarium

(c) Current Assets

(d) (i) • Annual General Meeting once a year – all members may attend
        • For election of office bearers
        • To consider accounts
        • Plan for future
        • To make decisions
    (ii) • When expenditure greater than income
         • Reduces accumulated fund
         • Loss by a club
         • Opposite of a surplus
         • A debit balance in P&L
    (iii) • What the club is worth
          • Assets – liabilities
          • Similar to capital
          • The members' interest in the club
          • Surpluses built up

(e) **Who?**
    • Club Official
    • Member of committee
    • Treasurer
    • Secretary
    • Volunteer worker

    Why?
    • Voluntary work for club
    • A thank you for work done
    • A gift / thank you

4. (a)

Chart Letter	Chart Name or Label
A	Sales or Total Revenue
B	Total Costs
C	Fixed Costs
D	Break Even Point
X	Output Quantity/Units
Y	Cost/Sales/Revenue/Income

(b)

Units	Fixed Costs	Variable Costs	Revenue	Profit/Loss
0	£200	0	0	(£200)
100	£200	£100	£200	(£100)
200	£200	£200	£400	0
300	£200	£300	£600	£100

(c) (i) Cost remains the same/does not vary as output/sales change
    (ii) • Costs which are not fixed
         • Cost changes/alters as the output/sales change
    (iii) • Where total cost is the same as total revenue.
          • Point (output/sales) at which no profit or loss is made.
          • Point at which above profits are made or below this point a loss is made.

5. (a) (i) $\dfrac{£10,000 + £6000}{2} = £8000$

    (ii) $\dfrac{£56,000}{£8000} = 7$ times

    (iii) $\dfrac{£24,000}{£80,000} \times \dfrac{100}{1} = 30.0\%$

    (iv) $\dfrac{£10,000}{£80,000} \times \dfrac{100}{1} = 12.5\%$

(b) Any two from:
    • Current (or Working Capital)
    • Acid Test
    • Return on Capital Invested

(c) Helios

(d) Any one from:
    • More advertising
    • Lower selling price
    • Location
    • Bulk buying discounts
    • Holding less stock
    • Special offers
    • Cheaper suppliers
    • Improved purchasing policy
    • Different industries or size of business
    • More sales

(e) Any one from:
    • Reduce expenses
    • Increase selling price
    • Reduce cost of sales
    • Find a cheaper supplier
    • Increase in GP%

6. (a)

	Debit	Credit
Capital - Tele		26,050
Capital - Machas		26,050
Drawings - Tele	2,000	
Drawings - Machas	1,000	
Bank Overdraft		2,400
Debtors	800	
Sales		10,000
Sales Returns	500	
Purchases	5,600	
Rent	100	
Creditors		5,000
Discount Received		500
Equipment	60,000	
	£70,000	£70,000

(b) Any one from:
- Check accuracy of double entry
- Assist/prepare final accounts
- Check Debits equals Credits
- An arithmetic check
- Errors may be noted and picked up

(c) Any three from:
- Additional partners
- Ploughing back profits
- Bank loan
- Mortgage
- Grant (not lottery)
- Introduce more capital or personal savings
- Venture capital

(d) Any three from:
- Error of Omission or Complete transaction missed out
- Error of Commission or Entry in wrong debtor/creditor account
- Error of Principle or Entry in wrong class of account
- Error of Original Entry or Error in Dr and Cr side
- Compensating Error or One error compensating for another on the opposite side
- Error of Complete Reversal or both entries entered the wrong way round, ie the Dr on the Cr and the Cr on the Dr
- If a transaction was entered twice

ACCOUNTING & FINANCE CREDIT 2007

1. (a)

INVOICE

The Bill Jones Garden Centre

53 Tinto Firs Road
GLASGOW
G15 7YZ

Telephone: 0141 944 4442   email: bjonesgc@htp.co.uk

Fax: 0141 944 2444   VAT Number: 1543 236

Invoice Number: 1225   Date: 13 April 2007

To: Gerry Tait
245 Coastal Lane
KILMARNOCK
KA1 4RS

Terms: 5% one month

Quantity	Description	Unit Price £ p	Cost £ p
4	Wooden Garden Chairs	25 00	100 00
1	Octagonal Garden Table	50 00	50 00
			150 00
	Less Trade Discount (10%)		15 00
	Net Goods Value		135 00
	Add VAT (17·5%)		22 44
	TOTAL		157 44
	Add Delivery		5 00
	AMOUNT DUE		162 44

VAT calculation: £135.00 − 6.75 = 128·25 × 17.5% = £22.44

(b) (i)
- customer loyalty
- bulk buying
- new customers

(ii)
- debtors to pay quickly
- help cash flow

(c) Cheque
- for payment of amounts outstanding

Statement
- to let customers know how much is owed
- to show details of all transactions during the month

Debit Note
- sent if a customer has been undercharged
- increase amount owing by customer

Receipt/Till roll slip
- sent to acknowledge payment
- acts as proof of payment

Credit Note
- when goods are returned
- when customer overcharged
- reduces amount owed
- states reason for return
- shows details of goods returned

2. (a) and (b)

Purchases Account

DATE	DETAILS	DR	CR	BAL
01/03/07	Balance	2,450·00		2,450·00 dr
02/03/07	Bank	100·00		2,550·00 dr
04/03/07	Drawings		200·00	2,350·00 dr

Sales Account

DATE	DETAILS	DR	CR	BAL
01/03/07	Balance		4,500·00	4,500·00 cr

A Black Account

DATE	DETAILS	DR	CR	BAL
01/03/07	Balance		600·00	600·00 cr
03/03/07	Purchase Returns & VAT	58·75		541·25 cr
05/03/07	Bank	505·00		36·25 cr
05/03/07	Discount Received	36·25		

Bank Account

DATE	DETAILS	DR	CR	BAL
01/03/07	Balance	2,700·00		2,700·00 dr
02/03/07	Purchases & VAT		117·50	2,582·50 dr
05/03/07	A Black		505·00	2,077·50 dr

VAT Account

DATE	DETAILS	DR	CR	BAL
02/03/07	Bank	17·50		17·50 dr
03/03/07	A Black		8·75	8·75 dr

Purchases Returns Account

DATE	DETAILS	DR	CR	BAL
03/03/07	A Black		50·00	50·00 cr

Drawings Account

DATE	DETAILS	DR	CR	BAL
04/03/07	Purchases	200·00		200·00 dr

Discount Received Account

DATE	DETAILS	DR	CR	BAL
05/03/07	A Black		36·25	36·25 cr

(c)
- A Suspense Account is required when a Trial balance fails to agree and the errors cannot be found. This allows the preparation of the final accounts to go ahead.
- The difference on the trial balance is entered in the Suspense account on Dr or Cr side in order for the Trial Balance to balance.
- It is recorded in the Balance Sheet – a Dr balance is a current asset/a Cr balance a current liability.
- Errors are corrected in the ledger account involved and the Suspense account.
- When all errors are found the Suspense account will have a zero balance and is closed.

(d) Jim could form a Partnership which would:
- provide extra capital
- provide expertise
- provide ideas
- provide borrowing power
- shared responsibility
- shared workload
- shared decision making
- shared losses

or Jim could form a Ltd or plc which would:
- provide extra capital (share and debenture issue)
- provide expertise of Board of Directors
- provide limited liability
- provide increased borrowing power
- ease of raising additional capital
- continuity of business.

or Jim could obtain a franchise:
- Selling well known products - higher sales possible.
- Advice from Franchisor (avoids mistakes relating to purchases or sales).
- (May get a loan easier) because franchise name is well known.
- Franchisor will advertise the business which will reduce overheads.
- Franchise business has more chance of success.

(e) Disadvantages of a partnership (any two from):
- loss of control
- partnership ceases on death of partner
- shared profit
- disagreements
- unlimited liability
- limited capital
- responsible for actions of other partners.

Disadvantages of a PLC (any two from):
- loss of sole ownership
- shared profit
- set up expenses high
- need to publish accounts
- loss of day to day control
- more legal considerations
- conflicts between Shareholder and Board of Directors.

Disadvantages of a franchise: (any two from):
- Must hand back % of profit in commission.
- Some franchises are very expensive to set up.
- No freedom in running the business the way you want.

3. (a) (i) Updated Bank Account

Date	Details	Dr £	Cr £	Bal £
30/3/07	Balance	2,020		2,020 dr
30/3/07	SO - Insurance		120	1,900 dr
30/3/07	Correction of error		90	1,810 dr
30/3/07	DD - Electricity		156	1,654 dr
30/3/07	BGC - Dividends	500		2,154 dr
30/3/07	Bank Charges		60	2,094 dr

(ii) **Bank Reconciliation Statement**
  For the month of March 2007

		£
Bank Statement Balance		1,739
LESS UNPRESENTED CHEQUES		
Postages	50	
Repairs	45	95
		1,644
ADD ITEMS NOT YET CREDITED		
Sales		450
Updated Bank Account Balance		**£2,094**

(b) *Any one from:*
- the amount involved can change each time
- the date of payment can change each time
- the person being paid informs bank of amount due
- more flexible
- cost is lower.

(c) *Any one from:*
- for use of bank's services (DD, SO, BGC, Cheques etc)
- customer going into overdraft
- to make a profit
- safe-keeping of money/valuables.

(d) *Any three from:*
- preference shares receive a fixed dividend/ordinary shares dividend varies
- preference share dividends are paid before ordinary share dividends
- in event of bankruptcy preference shares are refunded first
- ordinary shares carry voting rights
- preference shares are less risky than ordinary shares.

4. (a) **Appropriation Account**
   For year ended 30 April 2007

	£	£	£
NET PROFIT			90,000
LESS APPROPRIATIONS			
Transfer to General Reserve		18,000	
Interest on Capital			
Janet	10,000		
Jim	20,000	30,000	
Salary - Jim		6,000	54,000
RESIDUAL PROFIT			36,000
Share of Profit			
Janet		12,000	
Jim		24,000	
		£36,000	

(b) **Current Account – Jim Anderson**

		DR	CR	BAL
01/05/06	Balance	500		500 dr
30/04/07	Drawings	6,000		6,500 dr
30/04/07	Interest on Capital		20,000	13,500 cr
30/04/07	Salary		6,000	19,500 cr
30/04/07	Share of Profit		24,000	43,500 cr

(c) *Any one from:*
- as it is a way of reducing the profits available for distribution and therefore keeping funds in the business
- as it makes funds available to meet unforeseen events or for paying off debts
- as money can be transferred FROM the reserve if profits are low
- funds for expansion.

(d) *Any one from:*
- he works longer hours than Janet
- Jim is an Active partner
- he has extra skills/expertise
- he acts as the 'keyholder' for the business
- he carries out extra duties
- he is in the agreement.

(e) *Any two from:*
- the amount of capital invested (capital account) remains fixed whilst the owners' interest (capital + current account) in the company varies with time.
- If capital is to be used as the profit-sharing basis it cannot be allowed to change on a daily basis.
- The current account represents the floating capital the partner has in the business and can therefore be withdrawn freely.
- Current account shows changes due to profit/loss, salaries, drawings, interest.
- If the Capital Account remains fixed it allows the calculation of interest on Capital.

(f) *Any two sources and one relevant advantage/disadvantage from:*

Personal Savings/Invest More Capital
Advantages
- instant access to cash
- does not have to be repaid
- easy to arrange

Disadvantages
- more risk for owners
- heavier commitment
- opportunity cost

Government /EU grant (NOT lottery)
Advantages
- instant access to cash
- does not have to be repaid
- no interest payments

Disadvantages
- may have to meet certain requirements
- may not get all finance required
- may take a long time to arrange

Form PLC/Issue shares
Advantages
- instant access to cash
- does not have to be repaid
- remains permanently in the business
- dividends only paid if sufficient profits

Disadvantages
- profits have to be shared amongst more people
- more people have a say in the running of the business
- once authorised capital has been issued this source is closed

Mortgage/Remortgage

Advantages
- instant access to cash
- repaid over a number of years
- no loss of control of business
- easy and quick to arrange
- access to a large sum of money
- cost of repayment known

Disadvantages
- regular repayments required
- interest has to be paid
- additional expenses
- must be repaid

Take on New Partner(s)

Advantages
- more capital
- instant access to cash
- does not have to be repaid
- no interest payments
- remains permanently in business

Disadvantages
- have to share profit
- loss of control

Retain Profits

Advantages
- does not have to be repaid
- no interest payments
- no cost

Disadvantages
- less share of profit

5. (a) Current Ratio:
= Current Assets : Current Liabilities
= 6,600 : 2,200 = 3 : 1

Return on Capital Invested:
= Net Profit/Capital at beginning × 100
= 10,000/40,000 × 100 = **25%**

Acid Test Ratio:
= Current Assets − Stock : Current Liabilities
= 6,600 − 2,500 : 2,200 = 4,100 : 2,200
= 1.86 : 1

(b) Gross Profit % = GP/Sales × 100

Any one from:
- Shows % profit being made from buying/selling stock
- Can show if Selling Price needs to be increased
- Shows how well business is doing
- Can be compared to previous years/other businesses

Rate of Stock Turnover
= Cost of Sales/Average Stock

Any one from:
- Shows how quickly stock is being sold.
- Can avoid build up of stock.
- Lets you know how quickly to reorder.

Net profit % = NP/Sales × 100

Any one from:
- Shows how profitable the company is after expenses have been deducted.
- Can indicate changes in GP%.

(c)
- Businesses dealing in credit will occasionally suffer bad debts:
- Creating a Provision for Bad Debts is a way of anticipating/making an allowance for this.
- Debtors in the balance sheet more realistic.
- Net Profit is altered to a more realistic figure.
- The balance sheet total is reduced to a more realistic figure.

(d) *Any two from:*
- the owner has taken too much out in Drawings
- the business made a Loss
- the owner has withdrawn some of their capital.

6. (a) **Lucy Liu**

Cash Budget for Month of September 2007

	£	£
Opening Balance		13,000
ADD CASH IN		
Sales: Cash	4,000	
Credit	6,000	
Bank Loan	12,000	22,000
		35,000
LESS CASH OUT		
Purchase	8,000	
Rent	2,400	
Salaries	2,500	
Other Costs	3,000	
Equipment	15,000	30,900
Closing Balance		**£4,100**

(b) *Any one from:*
- highlight cash flow problems
- can predict future cash surpluses and arrange payment of debts/purchase of assets
- can predict future cash shortages and arrange overdrafts/loans
- you know your opening/closing balances; cash inflows/outflows
- you can plan for the future
- can be used to support applications for loans/show prospective investors
- allows you to set targets/goals

(c) *Any two from:*
- high volume of sales on credit
- high volume of purchases paid in cash whilst selling on credit
- money spent on acquiring fixed assets
- money spent on paying off debts
- high quantity of prepaid expenses/accrued expenses
- Drawings
- Capital income received

(d)
- Revenue expenditure is when money is spent on the day-to-day running of the organisation; it will usually be used up within one year. Affects profits.
- Capital expenditure is when money is spent on items that will increase the profit-making ability of the business; it is an investment in the business and will usually last longer than a year.

ACCOUNTING & FINANCE GENERAL 2008

1. *(a)*

```
                    Invoice
                  Elmer Gantry
                2 Princess Street
                   EDINBURGH
                     E4 5VR

Telephone: 0131 45692      Email: elmer@coolmail.co.uk
Fax: 0131 45692            VAT Number: 23245
To: Sinclair Lewis         Date: 30 April 2008
    12 Cathedral Street
    GLASGOW
    G28 3BY
```

Quantity	Description	Unit Price		Total	
		£	p	£	p
5	Staplers	8	00	40	00
2	Filing cabinets	100	00	200	00
				240	00
	Less 20% Trade Discount			48	00
	Net Goods Value			192	00
	Add VAT @ 17·5%			33	60
	TOTAL VALUE			**£225**	**60**

(b) Any one from:
- VAT must be paid to custom & excise/government
- Know how much to reclaim so can be recorded in ledger
- It is a tax adding to the cost of the goods
- It increases the selling price

(c) (i)
- Purchases
- VAT
- Elmer Gantry

(ii)
- Sales
- VAT
- Sinclair Lewis

(d) (i) *Any one from:*
- Encourages customers to buy in bulk and return again
- Increases sales

(ii) *Any one from:*
- Purchases cheaper
- More competitive
- Allows Lewis to make a profit/higher profit

(e) **Name:** Cash Discount

Purpose: Encourages prompt payment

2. *(a)* (i) and (ii) **Ledger of Richard Dawkins**

Account Name		**Bank**					
Date	Details	Dr		Cr		Balance	
		£	p	£	p	£	p
1 April	Balance			100	00	100	00
19 April	Daniel Dennet			273	75	373	75

Account Name		**Purchases**					
Date	Details	Dr		Cr		Balance	
		£	p	£	p	£	p
2 April	Daniel Dennet	400	00			400	00

Account Name		**VAT**					
Date	Details	Dr		Cr		Balance	
		£	p	£	p	£	p
2 April	Daniel Dennet	70	00			70	00
12 April	Daniel Dennet			26	75	43	75

Account Name		**Daniel Dennet**					
Date	Details	Dr		Cr		Balance	
		£	p	£	p	£	p
2 April	Purchases/VAT			470	00	470	00
12 April	Purchases Ret/VAT	176	25			293	75
19 April	Bank	273	75			20	00
19 April	Discount Received	20	00			-	-

Account Name		**Purchases Returns**					
Date	Details	Dr		Cr		Balance	
		£	p	£	p	£	p
12 April	Daniel Dennet			150	00	150	00

Account Name		**Discount Received**					
Date	Details	Dr		Cr		Balance	
		£	p	£	p	£	p
19 April	Daniel Dennet			20	00	20	00

(b) A Trial Balance

(c) Any three from:
- Limited capital
- Unlimited liability/unlimited debts
- Responsible for all losses
- Difficulty in arranging time off/holidays
- Heavy workload
- Sole responsibility for decisions
- Difficulty in borrowing
- If he dies business stops trading

(d) (i) **Trading Account**
- To calculate gross profit or gross loss
- To see how well business doing/buying and selling/making profit
- To calculate ratios
- See if he has made a profit

(ii) **Profit and Loss Account**
- To calculate net profit or net loss
- Overall profit to see how well business doing after expenses

(iii) **Balance Sheet**
- To present position of business
- Show assets, liabilities and capital
- To show how business is financed
- Shows business liquidity position

3. (a) (i) Updated Bank Account

Bank Account							
Date	Details	Dr		Cr		Balance	
		£	p	£	p	£	p
30 April	Balance	1,800	00			1,800	00
	Direct Debit - Book Club			160	00	1,640	00
	Standing Order - Hire of Room			5	00	1,635	00

(ii) **Bank Reconciliation Statement on 30 April 2008**

	£	£
Balance as per Bank Statement		1,725
Less unpresented cheques:		
Exhibition Hall	310	
Amazin Books	80	
		390
		1,335
Add lodgements – members		300
Updated Bank Balance		£1,635

(b) *Any two from:*
- Preparing accounts
- Present financial position at AGM
- Safe-keeping of money
- Giving financial advice

(c) (i) *Any one from:*
- No interest to pay
- Does not have to be repaid

(ii) *Any one from:*
- Time consuming
- Harder to get
- No guarantee of success
- Conditions may apply
- You do not get full amount
- Red tape

(d) *Any two from:*
- Any acceptable expense eg rent, honorarium, electricity, depreciation, book club, general expenses etc
- Any loss eg raffle

4. (a) (i) Current (Working Capital) Ratio

Current Assets : Current Liabilities
10,000 : 5,000
2 : 1

(ii) Return on Capital Invested

$$\frac{\text{Net Profit}}{\text{Opening Capital}} \times \frac{100}{1} = \frac{9,000}{76,000} \times \frac{100}{1} = 11 \cdot 8\%$$

(b) *Any two from:*
- Gross Profit Ratio
- Net Profit Ratio
- Rate of Stock Turnover Ratio
- Mark up Ratio
- Expenses Ratio

(c) **Partnership** *(any two from)*:
- 2-20 owners.
- Profits/losses shared.
- Unlimited liability.
- Partnership agreement.
- Specialisation.
- Easier to arrange time off.
- Greater capital than sole trader.
- Sleeping partner.

Public Limited Company (plc) *(any two from)*:
- Owners unlimited.
- Limited liability.
- More capital than sole trader and partnership.
- Ownership and management split.
- Owners are shareholders.
- Profits distributed as dividends.
- Debentures - long term liabilities.
- Pay corporation tax.
- Published accounts.
- AGM.
- Board of Directors.
- Different types of shares.
- Stock exchange.

Not-for-Profit organisation (eg club) *(any two from)*:
- Members are owners.
- Aim to provide service - not achieve profit.
- Committee elected at AGM
- Elected officials - usually voluntary
- Different terminology eg surplus, honorarium etc.
- Often receive financial assistance - grants from local autuorities etc.
- Run for good of community

(d) (i) **Capital Expenditure** *(any one from)*:
- Expenditure on fixed assets
- Spending on asset that will last more than one year

(ii) **Drawings** *(any one from)*:
- Reduction in capital
- Stock or cash taken by the owner for personal use

(iii) **Bad Debts** *(any one from)*:
- Debtors who have become bankrupt
- Debtor who does not pay
- Written off as expense in profit and loss account
- Debts which cannot be paid

(iv) **Counterfoil** *(any one from)*:
- Own record of cheques paid
- Document used for writing up accounts

(v) **Debtor** *(any one from)*:
- A current asset
- A person or business to whom goods have been sold on credit
- Someone who owes the business money
- Someone who is in debt

5. (a) A 12,000 − 4,000 = £8,000
B 4,000 + 1,000 = £5,000
C 60,000 + 40,000 = £100,000
D 10,000 + 2,000 = £12,000
E 2,000 − 5,000 = £3,000
F 120,000 − 80,000 = £40,000

(b) Decrease it

(c) *Any one from:*
- Cost of goods sold would be less
- Cost of purchases reduced

(d) *Any one from:*
- Less sales may be made
- People may buy elsewhere

6. (a) Appropriation Account of Adeneur & Kohl for the year ended 30 April 2008.

	£000s	£000s
Net Profit		85
Less Salary - Adeneur	15	
- Kohl	20	
		35
Residual profit		50
Share of profit:		
Adeneur	25	
Kohl	25	
		50

(b)

Adeneur - Current Account

Date	Details	Dr		Cr		Balance	
		£	p	£	p	£	p
30 April	Balance			5,000	00	5,000	00
	Share of Profit			25,000	00	30,000	00
	Drawings	10,000	00			20,000	00
	Salary			15,000	00	35,000	00

Kohl - Current Account

Date	Details	Dr		Cr		Balance	
		£	p	£	p	£	p
30 April	Balance	2,000	00			2,000	00
	Share of Profit			25,000	00	23,000	00
	Salary			20,000	00	43,000	00

(c) *Any one from:*
- Partnership Agreement/Contract/Deed
- Business plan

(d) *Any two from:*
- Death of a partner
- Bankrupt
- Partners agree to end
- Become plc
- Arguments
- Partnership may not make profit

ACCOUNTING & FINANCE CREDIT 2008

1. (a)
Statement of Account

Date	Details	Dr	Cr	Balance
		£	£	£
01/04	Balance	300.25		300.25 dr
10/04	Sales	262.40		562.65 dr
15/04	Payment/Bank		286.15	276.50 dr
	Discount		14.10	262.40 dr
19/04	Returns		52.48	209.92 dr

Working for 10/04

Goods	250.00
- Trade Discount – 10%	25.00
= NGV	225.00
+ VAT – 17.5%	37.40 *
= Total	£262.40
* NGV	225.00
- Cash Discount – 5%	11.25
	213.75
VAT – 17.5%	37.40

(b) 10/04 Invoice *(any one from)*:
- Sent by seller to buyer to indicate a credit sale
- Used by buyer to record in their accounts
- Allows buyer to check details
- Shows amount owed by buyer.

19/04 Credit Note *(any one from)*:
- Sent by seller to buyer to indicate return of goods bought on credit
- Used by buyer to record in their accounts
- States reason for the return
- Allows buyer to check details.

2. (a) (i) Bar Trading Account
For year ended 30/04/08

	£	£
Sales		52,334
Less Cost of Sales		
Opening Stock	2,950	
ADD purchases		
(25,000 − 225 + 350)	25,125	
	28,075	
LESS Closing Stock	1,890	26,185
GROSS PROFIT		26,149
Less Repairs to Bar	250	
Bar Wages (10,500 + 200)	10,700	10,950
Surplus/Profit on bar		£15,199

(ii) Income & Expenditure Accoun
For year ended 30/04/08

	£	£
Income		
Subscriptions		
(10,625 + 150 + 800)		11,575
Bar Profit		15,199
Donations		750
Competition Profit (900−475)		425
		27,949
Less Expenditure		
Honorarium	500	
Insurance	600	
Greenkeeper's Wages	6,000	
Depreciation of Equipment		
(12,500 + 1,500 − 13,000)	1,000	8,100
Surplus of Income over Expenditure		£19,849

(b) An Honorarium is a **gift** given to a **club official** in **recognition of the work done** for the club by them. It is **not a wage** and is **not based on hours worked** but reflects the fact that the work was **voluntary**.

(c) Any three sources/justifications from:
   Members levy
   - A compulsory one off payment by all club members
   - The finance would be raised quickly.
   Grant
   - No repayments required.
   - No interest payments
   Mortgage or Re-mortgage
   - Cash available quickly
   - Repayments over a long period
   - Low interest rates.
   Increase subscriptions
   - No repayments required
   - Members may be encouraged by better facilities
   Attract new members
   - No repayments required
   - Generates additional other income
   Increase entry fees
   - Long term increase in cash available
   Increase bar prices
   - As above
   Fundraisers
   - No repayments required
   Sponsorship
   - No repayments required
   Donations
   - No repayments required
   Sell Life Memberships
   - No repayments required

3. (a) Selling price = Sales/No of Units
   = 90,000/1,000 = £90

   Variable cost = Purchase/No of Units
   = 42,000/1,000 = £42

   Fixed costs = £30,000

   BEP = Fixed Costs/(SP−VC)

   30,000 / (90 − 42) = 625 bicycles

(b) New Fixed Cost = 30,000 − 10,080 = £19,920

   BEP = FC / Contribution

   19,920 / 48 = 415 bicycles

(c) Required Profit = £36,000

   (FC + RP)/Contribution = No of Units Required

   (19,920 + 36,000) / 48 = 1,165 bicycles

(d) A Fixed Cost is one that stays the same regardless of the level of activity.

   A Variable Cost is one that changes as the level of production changes.

(e) **Benefits** *(any two from)*:
   - More capital/expertise available.
   - Share of workload/losses/liabilities/debts.
   - Easier to take time off.
   - Greater borrowing power.

   Drawbacks *(any two from)*:
   - Have to share profits/decision making/control.
   - Possibility of disagreements.
   - Problems with death/retiral of partner.

4. (a) & (b)

BANK A/C

Date 2008	Details	Dr	Cr	Balance
01/05	Balance		350.00	350.00 cr
07/05	A Smith	55.00		295.00 cr

A SMITH A/C

Date 2008	Details	Dr	Cr	Balance
01/05	Balance	220.00		220.00 dr
07/05	Bank		55.00	165.00 dr
07/05	Bad Debts		165.0	0.00

G GREEN A/C

Date 2008	Details	Dr	Cr	Balance
01/05	Balance	424.00		424.00 dr
02/05	Sales & VAT	176.25		600.25 dr
10/05	Sales Returns & VAT		58.75	541.50 dr

VAT A/C

Date 2008	Details	Dr	Cr	Balance
01/05	Balance		110.00	110.00 cr
02/05	G Green		26.25	136.25 cr
10/05	G Green	8.75		127.50 cr

SALES A/C

Date 2008	Details	Dr	Cr	Balance
02/05	G Green		150.00	150.00 cr

BAD DEBTS A/C

Date 2008	Details	Dr	Cr	Balance
07/05	A Smith	165.00		165.00 cr

SALES RETURNS A/C

Date 2008	Details	Dr	Cr	Balance
10/05	G Green	50.00		50.00 dr

(c) • Create a Provision for Bad Debts
  • **P&L A/C** *(any one from)*:
    • The amount is entered in P&L A/C as an Expense/Income.
    • This will Reduce/Increase the Net Profit.
    • It reduces the profits available distribution.
  • **BALANCE SHEET** *(any one from)*:
    • The PBD is deducted from Debtors in the Balance Sheet.
    • This will reduce Current Assets/Working Capital/Balance Sheet Total.
    • It gives a more realistic Debtors figure in the Balance Sheet.

(d) He could set up a Petty Cash System using the Imprest System.

And any three from:
  • The Petty Cashier is given a cash "float" (the Imprest).
  • All small Cash receipts/payments are recorded in a Petty Cash Book/Statement.
  • Petty Cash Vouchers (PCV's) are used.
  • Payments are entered into analysis columns eg Postage, Stationery etc
  • The amount of cash paid out by the Petty Cashier is reimbursed at the end of the accounting period.
  • The totals of the analysis columns are posted to the relevant ledger accounts at the end of the accounting period.
  • Only the total cash issued to Petty Cash during the accounting period will appear in the Cash A/c.
  • This reduces the amount of entries in the Cash A/c as well as other Ledger A/cs.
  • Gives responsibility to a Junior member of staff.

5. (a)

Opening Stock + Purchases − Closing Stock = **Cost of Sales**
4,000 + 57,000 − 6,000 = **55,000**

Sales − Cost of Sales = **Gross Profit**
100,000 − 55,000 = **45,000**

Gross Profit − Expenses = **Net Profit**
45,000 − 25,000 = **20,000**

(Op St + Cl St)/2 = **Average Stock**
(4,000 + 6,000)/2 = **5,000**

GP% = GP/Sales × 100
45,000/100,000 × 100 = **45%**

NP% = NP/Sales × 100
20,000/100,000 = **20%**

Rate of Stockturn = COS/Av St
55,000/5,000 = **11 times**

(b) To improve Working Capital/(Current) Ratio:

Any two from:
  • Increase **current** assets.
  • Reduce **current** liabilities.
  • Put in more capital.
  • Obtain a long term loan.
  • Reduce drawings.
  • Sell Fixed Assets no longer required.

To improve the Return on Capital Invested Ratio:
Any two from:
  • Increase Selling Prices.
  • Improve sales/productivity/profit.
  • Cut costs/expenses/find cheaper supplier.
  • Diversify/sell products that give greater profit.
  • Rationalise/stop selling products that are unprofitable.

(c) *Any three from:*
  • Future planning.
  • Compare business with others.
  • Compare performance with previous years.
  • To see how well the business is doing.
  • Compare with industry average.
  • Highlight areas of concern.
  • Show potential investors.
  • Use at AGM.
  • Can take action before situation deteriorates irretrievably.

(d) *Any three from:*
  • Ordinary shares receive a Dividend/Debenture holders receive interest.
  • The rate of Dividend is variable/rate of interest is fixed.
  • The rate of Dividend is dependant on profit/rate of Interest unaffected by profits.
  • Shares form part of Capital/Debentures are Long Term Liabilities.
  • Shareholders own part of the company/ Debenture holders are secured creditors.
  • Ordinary Shareholders have voting rights/Debenture holders do not.
  • Shares can be bought and sold when convenient/Debentures are paid back at a specific time.
  • In the event of bankruptcy Ordinary Shareholders could lose their investment/Debentures would not.
  • In the event of bankruptcy Debenture holders are paid out first/Ordinary shareholders are paid last.

6. (a) The Suspense Account

(b) *Any one from (maximum of 4)*:
  • error of omission
  • document missed out
  • transaction missed out.

Plus

Any one from:
  • No debit or credit entries have been made therefore TB will still balance
  • eg if an invoice is lost no entries are made in the Sales/VAT/Debtors A/c's.

Any one from:
  • error of original entry
  • error taking figures from original document.

Plus

Any one from:
  • The wrong figure is taken from the original document and both Dr and Cr are carried out using this figure
  • eg cheque for £245 is recorded in Dr and Cr as £254.

Any one from:
  • error of principle
  • transaction entered in wrong class of account.

Plus

Any one from:
  • Sale of an Asset is recorded in Sales A/c instead of Asset A/c
  • Dr and Cr are still equal so TB balances.

Any one from:
  • error of commission
  • transaction recorded in the correct class of account but the wrong one.

Plus

Any one from:
  • Payment of expenses recorded in wrong expense account
  • eg payment for Wages entered in Salaries A/c.

Any one from:
- complete reversal
- entries round wrong way but in correct accounts.

Plus

Any one from:
- Account which should have been Dr is Cr while the account that should have Cr is Dr
- eg payment by cheque for petrol is entered as Dr Bank A/c and Cr Petrol A/c.

Any one from:
- compensating errors
- where one error is cancelled out by one or more other errors

Plus
- eg Purchases A/c Dr £100 in error and Sales A/c Cr £100 in error.

ACCOUNTING & FINANCE GENERAL 2009

1. (a)

QUAN-TITY	DESCRIPTION	UNIT PRICE £	COST £
3	Operator Chairs	60.00	180.00
1	Cross-cut Shredder	20.00	20.00
			200.00
	Less 10% Trade Discount		20.00
	Net Goods Value		180.00
	Add VAT @17.5%		31.50
	TOTAL		£211.50

(b)
- Equipment/Furniture/Fixtures Account
- VAT Account
- Grove Office Supplies

(c) (i) • Trade Discount is a reduction in the price of goods

(ii) *Any one from:*
- Bulk buying
- To encourage customers to return
- To encourage new customers
- Given to trade/regular/loyal customers
- Allow them to make a profit

(d) *Any two from:*
- Faulty
- Wrong size/colour/item sent
- Damaged/broken
- Found goods cheaper at another supplier
- Ordered too many
- Unsuitable

(e) *Any one from:*
- No need for cash
- Pay at a later date
- Pay in instalments
- Time to sell before paying
- Improves cash flow

2. (a)

Account Name		Sales				Number 1	
Date	Details	Dr		Cr		Balance	
		£	p	£	p	£	p
02/03/09	Food 2 U			90	00	90	00

Account Name		VAT				Number 2	
Date	Details	Dr		Cr		Balance	
		£	p	£	p	£	p
02/03/09	Food 2 U			15	75	15	75
18/03/09	Food 2 U	6	30			9	45

Account Name		FOOD 2 U				Number 3	
Date	Details	Dr		Cr		Balance	
		£	p	£	p	£	p
02/03/09	Sales and VAT	105	75			105	75
18/03/09	Sales Returns and VAT			42	30	63	45
22/03/09	Bad Debts			63	45	00	00

Account Name		Sales Returns				Number 4	
Date	Details	Dr		Cr		Balance	
		£	p	£	p	£	p
18/03/09	Food 2 U	36	00			36	00

Account Name		Bad Debts				Number 5	
Date	Details	Dr		Cr		Balance	
		£	p	£	p	£	p
22/03/09	Food 2 U	63	45			63	45

(b) *Any two from*:
- It gives a record of the month's transactions
- It shows closing balances **or**
- It shows how much is still owed
- It shows when payment is due
- It shows purchases and returns/invoices and credit notes/payments and discounts

(c) *Any two from*:
- More capital/money
- Additional expertise/skills
- Greater borrowing power
- Shared losses
- Shared workload
- Shared decision making
- Specialisation
- Easier to take time off/holidays
- More ideas
- Bring more contacts

(d) • The owners personal possessions could be sold/taken/lost to cover business debts if the business fails

3. (a)

JS Technologies plc Trial Balance as at 31 March 2009		
	DR	CR
Wages and Salaries	146,000	
Debtors	44,000	
Purchases	291,000	
Bank	27,000	
Debentures		30,000
Sales Returns	1,500	
Discount Allowed	1,250	
Ordinary Shares		88,000
Premises	160,000	
Stock	22,750	
Discount Received		1,500
Creditors		30,000
Sales		534,000
Unappropriated Profit		10,000
	£693,500	£693,500

(b) *Any two from*:
- To check accuracy of ledger
- To check double entry
- To check that DR = CR
- Errors may be picked up
- Arithmetic check of the ledger
- To allow Final Accounts to be prepared
- To see if Suspense Account is required

(c)

Description of Error	Name of Error
A transaction has been completely missed out.	**Omission**
The account which should have been debited is credited and the account which should have been credited is debited.	**Reversal**
The wrong type of account has been used eg Purchases Account instead of Equipment Account.	**Principle**
The correct accounts were used but the wrong figure entered eg £345 entered instead of £453.	**Original Entry**
Two or more errors have cancelled each other out.	**Compensating**

4. (a) **THE MAGIC CARPET STORE**

Trading and Profit and Loss Accounts for the year ended 30 April 2009

	£	£	£
Sales			124,500
Less: Sales Returns			2,700
			121,800
Less Cost of Sales			
Opening Stock		8,000	
Purchases		80,200	
Carriage In		1,600	
		89,800	
Less Closing Stock		7,400	82,400
GROSS PROFIT			39,400
Add Rent Received			4,400
			43,800
Less Expenses			
Insurance (9,600 − 1,600)		8,000	
Wages (6,400 + 580)		6,980	
Advertising		5,600	
Carriage Out		730	
Depreciation – Furniture		2,500	23,810
(10% × 25,000)			
NET PROFIT			£19,990

(b) (i) • Short term debt
  • What is owed by a firm short term eg creditors, bank overdraft

(ii) • Cash/goods which the owner of the business takes out for their own use

(c) *Any two from*:
  • To record small items of expenditure eg stamps, milk, tea etc
  • To help reduce book-keeping errors
  • To keep cheques for large amounts
  • To stop ledger accounts getting cluttered
  • To reduce the workload of the cashier
  • To give a junior more responsibility

5. (a) (i) The Gross Profit Percentage

$$\frac{£3,750}{£15,000} \times \frac{100}{1} = 25\%$$

(ii) The Rate of Stock Turnover

$$\frac{1,050 + 1,200}{2} = \frac{2,250}{2} = £1,125$$

$$\frac{£11,250}{£1,125} = 10 \text{ times}$$

(b) *Any two from*:
  • Future planning
  • To compare with previous years
  • To compare with other similar organisations/businesses
  • To see how well the club is doing
  • Explanation of using specific ratio

(c) *Any one from*:
  • Reduce cost of sales
  • Cheaper supplier
  • Bulk buy at lower prices
  • Obtain discounts
  • Reduce waste/theft
  • Increase selling price

(d) (i) *Any one from*:
  • Amount paid annually/weekly/monthly by members to use facilities
  • Membership fee
  • Main source of income for organization

(ii) *Any one from*:
  • When income is greater than expenditure
  • Increases accumulated fund
  • Profit of a club
  • Opposite of a deficit
  • Similar to a profit in a business

(iii) *Any one from*:
  • What the club is worth
  • Assets − Liabilities
  • Similar to capital
  • Capital
  • The members interest in the club
  • Surpluses built up

(e) *Any two from*:
  • Opening balance/Closing balances
  • Capital income/expenditure
  • Fixed Assets
  • Any Fixed Asset examples
  • Capital Income examples eg mortgage, loan
  • Any Bar Trading items
  • Loan/Long-term Liabilities

(f) *Any two from*:
  • Donations
  • Mortgage
  • Grant
  • Fund raising events
  • Attract additional members
  • Sponsorship
  • (Bank) loan
  • Levy on members
  • Charge non members
  • Sell assets

6. (a)

	July £	August £
OPENING BALANCE	3,800	3,400
Receipts		
Credit Sales	1,500	1,820
	5,300	5,220
Payments		
Purchase	1,100	1,220
Wages	600	600
Insurance	200	200
Production Equipment	0	1,500
	1,900	3,520
CLOSING BALANCE	£3,400	£1,700

(b) *Any one from*:
  • Helps planning
  • Identifies potential shortfall
  • Arrange loan/overdraft if required
  • Identifies potential surplus
  • Gives closing balances
  • Shows cash in/cash out
  • Shows when costs need to be cut/savings made
  • Shows when something can be afforded
  • Helps cash flow

(c) *Any one from*:

Debentures
- long term loans
- interest payable at a fixed rate
- amount repaid in total
- long-term liabilities shown in Balance Sheet

Any one from:
Unappropriated Profit
- balance at start/balance at end of Appropriation A/c
- profit at year end not distributed
- shown in Balance Sheet as reserve
- profit left after paying dividends

(d) *Any one from*:
- The directors decide the percentage rate
- Profits can vary
- High profit more dividend/low profit less dividend
- More shares issued
- Business makes a loss

(e) (i) • Number of shares that can be issued/sold

(ii) • Number of shares which a company has issued/sold

ACCOUNTING & FINANCE CREDIT 2009

1. (a)

Account Name: Bank

Date	Details	Dr		Cr		Balance	
		£	p	£	p	£	p
1 May	Balance			1,000	00	1,000	00
12 May	Equipment/Faraday			2,000	00	3,000	00
18 May	Repairs/VAT			141	00	3,141	00

Account Name: Equipment

Date	Details	Dr		Cr		Balance	
		£	p	£	p	£	p
1 May	Balance	5,500	00			5,500	00
12 May	Faraday	8,000	00			13,500	00
22 May	Faraday			80	00	13,420	00

Account Name: M Faraday – Creditor

Date	Details	Dr		Cr		Balance	
		£	p	£	p	£	p
1 May	Balance			800	00	800	00
12 May	Equipment/VAT			7,400	00	8,200	00
22 May	Equipment/VAT	94	00			8,106	00

Account Name: M Faraday – Creditor

Date	Details	Dr		Cr		Balance	
		£	p	£	p	£	p
1 May	Balance			800	00	800	00
12 May	Equipment/VAT			9,400	00	10,200	00
12 May	Bank	2,000	00			8,200	00
22 May	Equipment/VAT	94	00			8,106	00

Account Name: VAT

Date	Details	Dr		Cr		Balance	
		£	p	£	p	£	p
7 May	Lavoiser	35	00			35	00
12 May	Faraday	1,400	00			1,435	00
18 May	Bank	21	00			1,456	00
22 May	Faraday			14	00	1,442	00

Account Name: Purchases

Date	Details	Dr		Cr		Balance	
		£	p	£	p	£	p
7 May	Lavoiser	200	00			200	00

Account Name: Lavoiser – Creditor							
Date	Details	Dr		Cr		Balance	
		£	p	£	p	£	p
7 May	Purchases/VAT			235	00	235	00

Account Name: Repairs							
Date	Details	Dr		Cr		Balance	
		£	p	£	p	£	p
18 May	Bank	120	00			120	00

(b) *Any one from*:
- For every debit there is a credit entry
- For each transaction the total debited should be the same as the total credited

(c) (i) • This would be much greater/more money (potentially) as a plc as there are far more individuals to invest in the business

(ii) *Any one from*:
- Borrowing may be easier to arrange with banks
- Borrowing may be cheaper – lower rate of interest if borrowing a larger amount
- Greater variety of borrowing is possible – eg debentures, long term borrowing
- A larger sum may be borrowed

(iii) *Any one from*:
- Unlike a partnership liability is limited
- Shareholders would only lose at most their share holding in the plc
- Partners' personal assets are at risk in the event of bankruptcy but not in the case of a plc

2. (a)

Account Name: Moore Motors							
Date	Details	Dr		Cr		Balance	
		£	p	£	p	£	p
1 May	Balance	500	00			500	00
7 May	Sales	887	98			1,387	98
21 May	Sales Returns			90	00	1,297	98
28 May	Bank			470	00	827	98
28 May	Discount			30	00	797	98

(b) *Any one from*:

Advantage
- Develop customer loyalty
- A greater number of customers
- Encourages more sales

Any one from:

Disadvantage
- May cause cash flow problems
- Debtors may become bankrupt
- May lead to bad debts

(c) • Credit note
- Gross profit would fall

(d) *Any three from*:
- To explain why their own bank balance is different from that on the bank statement
- To ensure an error has not been made by the bank
- To ensure an error has not been made in your own bank account
- Owing to delays in the banking system – unpresented cheques and lodgements
- Items recorded on the bank statement but not included in the business' bank account eg standing order, direct debit, charges, BGC etc

3. (a) (i) Open the required account to make the Trial Balance agree

(ii)

Account Name: Suspense							
Date	Details	Dr		Cr		Balance	
		£	p	£	p	£	p
30 April	Balance			81	00	81	00
	Rent			63	00	144	00
	Discount Received	24	00			120	00
	B Skinner	120	00			-	

(b) • If the bank is an asset/there is money in the bank it will have a debit balance
- If it is an overdraft/money is owed to the Bank it will have a credit balance

(c) *Any two from*:
- Only revenue expenditure should be recorded
- Capital expenditure would give an unrealistic profit/loss figure
- It may lead to poor decisions – eg raising prices in the mistaken belief this is necessary as the business has a loss because it wrongly included capital expenditure
- Capital expenditure is recorded in the Balance Sheet
- Capital is expenditure on fixed assets which last longer than a year

(d)

Source	Advantage	Disadvantage
Grant (not lottery)	• Do not need to repay • No interest repayments	• Time consuming to apply • May not be successful • May have to wait a considerable time for response to application • Conditions may have to be met
Loan from family/friend	• Simple to arrange • Possibly greater flexibility in repaying • Possibly lower or no interest charge on loan	• Interest may have to be paid • Loan must be repaid • Could cause family/friend tensions about business
Mortgage/remortgage	• Relatively simple to arrange • Money can be made available relatively quickly • Cost of repayment known in advance • Could be spread over a longer period of time, eg 25 years • Access to a large sum of money	• Interest rate may be variable • Additional expense • Possible reduction in profits • Must be repaid • May not be enough
Personal savings	• Easy to arrange • No repayment costs	• Heavier commitment • Opportunity cost
Partnership	• Considerably larger capital possible • Do not need to repay	• Any profits will have to be shared • Time consuming to organise • Still unlimited liability
Plc	• Considerably larger capital possible • Do not need to repay • Limited liability	• Any profits will have to be shared • Time consuming to organise • Expensive to launch

4. (a) **Appropriation Account for year ended 30 April 2009**

	£000	£000
Net Profit		30
Add: Unappropriated Profit 1 May 2008		9
		39
Less:		
Interim Ordinary Dividend	1	
Proposed Preference Dividend	1	
Proposed Ordinary Dividend	2	4
Unappropriated Profit/Profit & Loss Account Balance 30 April 2009		£35

Balance Sheet as at 30 April 2009

	£000	£000 Cost	£000 Prov for dep	£000 NBV
Fixed Assets				
Vehicles		228	6	222
Current Assets				
Stock		5		
Debtors	22			
Less Prov for Bad Debts	3	19		
VAT		5		
Electricity paid in advance		4		
			33	
Less Current Liabilities				
Creditors	53			
Bank Overdraft	10			
Debenture Interest Owing	2			
Proposed Ord Dividend	2			
Proposed Pref Dividend	1			
Expenses owing	2			
			70	
Working Capital				(37)
				£185
Issued Share Capital				
10% Preference Shares				10
Ordinary Shares				100
				110
Reserves				
Profit & Loss Balance				35
				145
Long Term Liabilities				
5% Debentures				40
				£185

(b) (i) *Any one from*:
- Funds for expansion at no monetary cost
- No interest, or dividends have to be paid for profits retained
- To set aside resources for any unforeseen events
- To allow the purchase of fixed assets
- To reduce chance of liquidity problems

(ii) *Any one from*:

Advantage
- Expansion of business – potential higher profits
- Greater stability
- More profits available for distribution in future as dividends
- An increase in the share price – potential capital gains in the longer term – as a result of higher profits

Any one from:

Disadvantage
- Lower dividends in the short term
- Market value of shares may fall in the short term – if dividend is lower than expected
- If forced to sell shares a loss on capital invested may result

(c) *Any one Bad debt/Provision for Bad Debt from:*
- Bad debts are a past event – the money has been lost
- Provision for bad debts is an attempt to anticipate bad debts in the future
- Bad debts are an expense
- Provision for bad debts can be reduced; this adds to the profit
- Bad debts are always deducted from the profit
- Provision for bad debts is deducted from debtors in the balance sheet
- Bad debts do not appear in the balance sheet

5. (a)

	2008	2009
Current Ratio	12,000/5,000 = 2.4:1	8,000/7,000 = 1.14:1
RCI	$\frac{26,000}{80,000} \times 100$ = 32.5%	$\frac{26,000}{106,000} \times 100$ = 18.87%

(b) **Current Ratio**
- There has been a deterioration in the liquidity position
- Purchase of fixed assets
- Moved from a situation where current liabilities can be met with ease to one where it may be very difficult to meet them
- Current assets have dropped significantly; current liabilities have increased. This may be because of not keeping sufficient money in the bank to pay debts

RCI
- There has been a dramatic deterioration on the profit as a percentage of the capital invested at the start of the year
- Despite the business expanding (capital increasing by £26,000) the net profit has declined by £6,000
- This could have been caused by a number of factors: an increase in selling price resulting in a significant fall in sales; an increase in the cost of purchases and or expenses; a slow down in the economy; more competition etc

(c)
- *Gross profit ratio* informs the business how successful it is at buying and selling the product – compared to previous years and similar businesses; shows how much out of every £ of sales is profit
- *Net profit ratio* informs the business how successful it is at controlling its expenses – compared to previous years and similar businesses
- *Rate of stock turnover* informs the business how successful it has been at moving its stock – compared to previous years and similar businesses

(d) *Any two from:*
- The absolute net profit can be misleading
- What matters is the net profit relative to turnover and capital invested
- A small business may have a much higher net profit ratio and RCI than a much larger business. However the larger business' net profit may be significantly larger than that of the smaller business
- The business with the largest net profit may have liquidity problems
- Examples of the above points would be acceptable

6. (a) **Trading, Profit and Loss Account for year ended 30 April 2009**

	£	£
Sales		55,000
Less cost of Goods Sold		22,000
Gross Profit		33,000
Rent received		5,000
		38,000
Less Expenses	10,000	
Sales Bonus	500	
Bank Interest	160	
		10,660
Net Profit		£27,340

(b) • Cash Budget

Assist the business:
Any two from:
- Help them to decide when it would be an appropriate time to buy new fixed assets – to avoid creating any liquidity problems
- Identifies when it will be necessary to arrange a bank overdraft – this will allow it to be negotiated prior to the event
- To let them know opening and closing balances
- Identify when they are short of cash
- Identify what they spend too much on
- Can see estimated income and expenditure
- Help them consider when to cut down on purchases/expenses
- Shows money coming in/out of business
- Identify if cash resources are growing too high
- Allow consideration of how the funds can be employed more profitably

(c) (i) *Any one from:*
- The Receipts and Payments Account only contains cash/bank transactions
- Does not show adjustments for prepayments and accruals
- It gives no indication of profitability of Club (surplus/deficit)
- Does not show change in value of Fixed Assets
- Does not show what the Club is worth
- Does not cover all financial areas

(ii) *Any two statements and justification from:*

Refreshments/Bar Trading Account
- Shows whether Club Bar is making a profit/loss for financial period
- Decide if prices need to be increased
- See if worthwhile to continue running it

Fund-raising Income Statements
- Shows whether these events are making a profit/loss
- See if worthwhile doing again next year

Income and Expenditure Account
- Shows profit/loss from fund raising events or bar etc
- Contains all revenue income/expenditure for financial period, adjusted where necessary, for prepayments and accruals
- The Income and Expenditure Account shows if the Club has made a surplus/deficit

Balance Sheet/Statement of Affairs
- Shows what the Club is worth
- Shows Working Capital of Club
- Shows NBV of Club's Fixed Assets
- Shows the assets/liabilities of the Club

- Shows the amount of Accumulated Funds at the year end
- Shows the liquidity of the club

Cash Budget
- Help plan for the future
- Identify cash shortages
- Identify cash surpluses - when fixed assets could be bought
- Identify opening and closing balances
- Can see estimated income and expenditure
- Identify when to cut down on purchases/expenses

ACCOUNTING & FINANCE GENERAL 2010

1. (a)

Quantity	Description	Unit Price		Cost	
		£	p	£	p
3	Festival Flower tents	80	00	240	00
1	Camper lamp	10	00	10	00
				250	00
	Less 10% Trade Discount			25	00
	Net Goods Value			225	00
	Add VAT @ (17·5%)			39	37
	Total			**£264**	**37**

(b)
- Sales Returns A/c
- VAT A/c
- McCombie Camping A/c

(c) Name: Cash (Discount)
   Explanation: Encourages prompt payment
   Improves Cash Flow

(d)

	Document Name
McCombie Camping plc buys goods on credit from Canvas Creations	**Invoice**
Canvas Creations sends McCombie Camping plc a summary of their transactions for the month	**Statement (of Account)**
McCombie Camping plc pays £50 of the amount owed to Canvas Creations in cash	**Receipt**

2. (a) **Ledger of Gairneybank Garden Centre**

Account Name:	Bank				Number	1
Date	Details	Dr		Cr		Balance	
		£	p	£	p	£	p
14/4/2010	Balance	2,000	00			2,000	00
25/4/2010	Garden Sundries			400	00	1,600	00

Account Name:	Garden Sundries plc				Number	2
Date	Details	Dr		Cr		Balance	
		£	p	£	p	£	p
14/4/2010	Purchases and VAT			528	75	528	75
22/4/2010	Purchases Returns and VAT	94	00			434	75
25/4/2010	Bank	400	00			34	75

Account Name:	Purchases					Number 3	
Date	Details	Dr		Cr		Balance	
		£	p	£	p	£	p
14/4/2010	Garden Sundries	450	00			450	00

Account Name:	VAT					Number 4	
Date	Details	Dr		Cr		Balance	
		£	p	£	p	£	p
14/4/2010	Garden Sundries	78	75			78	75
22/4/2010	Garden Sundries			14	00	64	75

Account Name:	Purchases Returns					Number 5	
Date	Details	Dr		Cr		Balance	
		£	p	£	p	£	p
22/4/2010	Garden Sundries			80	00	80	00

(b) • Shareholders liability is limited to value of their investment
    or
   • Shareholders can't lose their personal possessions
    or
   • Shareholders have limited liability

(c) • Shareholders

(d) • Shares (can be issued)
   • Debentures (can be issued)

(e) *Any one from:*
   • Cash Budget
   • Cash Flow (Statement)

3. (a) (i) **Picture Perfect Photography Club**
Statement of Profit/Loss on Sale of Refreshments for the year ended 31 December 2009

	£	£
Sale of Refreshments		620
Less: Cost of Sales		
Opening Stock	500	
Add: Purchase of Refreshments	330	
	830	
Less: Closing Stock	320	
		510
Profit on Refreshments		£110

(ii) **Picture Perfect Photography Club**
Income and Expenditure Account for the year ended 31 December 2009

	£	£
Income		
Profit on Refreshments		110
Members Subscriptions		1,400
Donations		300
Grant		800
		£2,610

Expenditure

Insurance (85−15)	70	
Cleaner's Wages (165 + 80)	245	
Repairs to Premises	90	
Depreciation of Equipment*	435	840
Surplus		£1,770

* (1800 + 1100) × 15%

(b) *Any two from:*
   • Mortgage
   • Members Levy
   • Raise subscriptions
   • Increase membership
   • Fundraising
   • Loan
   • Sponsorship

(c) *Any two from:*
   • Wear and tear
   • Obsolescence
   • Age
   • Damaged/Broken
   • To provide realistic Balance Sheet figure
   • To provide realistic profit/surplus figure

(d) Accumulated Fund *(any one from)*:
   • What the club is worth
   • Assets−Liabilities
   • Similar to Capital
   • Surpluses built up

Subscriptions Prepaid *(any one from)*:
   • Subscriptions paid in any one accounting period but not due until the next accounting period
   • Subscriptions paid before they are due/in advance
   • A liability because they owe the membership

4. (a) Selling Price − Variable Costs = Contribution per Chair
$$£40 - (£20 + £3 + £2) = £15$$

(b) $$\frac{\text{Fixed Costs}}{\text{Contribution per chair}} = \text{Break Even Point}$$

$$\frac{(£800 + £500 + £200)}{£15} = 100 \text{ chairs}$$

(c)
$$\left(\begin{array}{c}\text{Total Number} \\ \text{Sold}\end{array} - \begin{array}{c}\text{Break Even} \\ \text{Sales}\end{array}\right) \times \begin{array}{c}\text{Contribution} \\ \text{per Chair}\end{array} = \text{Profit}$$

$$(120 - 100) \times £15 = £300$$

(d) *Any one from:*
   • (Partnership) Agreement
   • Deed
   • Contract

(e) *Any two from:*
   • Capital
   • Share of profits/losses
   • Drawings
   • Interest on drawings
   • Interest on Capital
   • Partners' salaries

(f) (i) *Any two from:*
   • Responsibility for all decisions/own boss/total control
   • Quicker decision making
   • Gets all of the profits
   • Easy to set up
   • Personal touch
   • Accounts kept private

(ii) *Any two from:*
- Limited capital
- Unlimited liability/unlimited debts
- Responsible for all losses
- Difficulty in arranging time off/holidays
- Heavy workload
- Sole responsibility for decisions
- Difficulty in borrowing
- If sole trader dies business stops trading
- Limited knowledge/expertise

5. (a)

Peter Canning
Trial Balance as at 31 January 2010

	Dr	Cr
	£	£
Sales		12,800
Wages	1,900	
Premises	8,000	
Sales Returns	260	
Drawings	3,600	
Rent Received		220
Debtors	580	
Purchases	7,000	
Capital		6,500
Bank Overdraft		3,400
Carriage Out	360	
Stock	1,220	
	£22,920	£22,920

(b) *Any two from:*
- To check double entry is complete
- To check if DR = CR
- Arithmetic check of Ledger Accounts
- Errors may be picked up from Ledger Accounts
- To aid preparation of final accounts
- To check ledger accuracy

(c) (i) • Increase both (totals by £200)
  Any one from:
  - DR Debtors A/c £200 and CR Sales A/c £200
  - Both DR and CR would have an extra entry

(ii) • No effect (on totals)
  Any one from:
  - Entry is on correct side of the wrong account ie DR
  - Correction would move entry from DR of Purchases Account to DR of Office Equipment Account
  - Correction would CR Purchases and DR Office Equipment

(d) *Any three from:*
- Gross Profit
- Mark up
- Net Profit
- Rate of Stock Turnover
- Expenses
- Acid Test

(e) (i) *Any one from:*
- Bank balance is CR
- Current Liability
- Happens when business spends more than they have in Bank Account

(ii) When the <u>owner(s)</u> of the business take(s) money/stock/services for <u>personal use</u>

6. (a) (i) CA : CL
      7,600 : 3,330
      2.28/2.3 : 1

(ii) $\dfrac{£4,600}{£23,870} \times \dfrac{100}{1} = 19\cdot27\%/19\cdot3\%$

(b) • (Trading and) Profit and Loss Account

(c) *Any two from:*
- Comparison to previous years
- Comparison to similar businesses
- Comparison to industry average
- Identify strengths/weaknesses
- To see if the business is efficient
- To aid planning
- To show potential investor/banks/suppliers
- To see how well the business is doing

ACCOUNTING & FINANCE CREDIT 2010

1. (a)

Quantity	Description	Unit Price		Cost	
		£	p	£	p
3	3M/25 mm Copper Piping	12	00	36	00
2	Copper Angle Joints	40	00	80	00
				116	00
	Less 10% Trade Discount			11	60
	Net Goods Value			104	40
	Add VAT (17·5%)*			17	35
	TOTAL			121	75
	Add Delivery			5	00
	AMOUNT DUE			**£126**	**75**

Working: NGV £104·40 * 5% CD = £5·22
£104·40 − £5·22 = £99·18
£99·18 * 17·5% VAT = £17·35

(b) *Any one from:*
Trade Discount is given to:
- Encourage to use our business
- Continue to use
- Attract new customers
- Retain loyal customers
- Encourage bulk buying

Any one from:
- Cash Discount is given to encourage prompt payment
- To help Cash Flow

(c) (i) • Credit Note

(ii) *Any one from:*
- As it was a credit transaction in the first place
- No money changed hands
- The Credit Note reduces the amount owed

(d) *Any two sources and justifications from:*

Source	Justification
Mortgage	Money received straight away
Remortgage	Repayments can be spread over a long period
Loans	Straightforward to arrange
Grant	No need to repay
Personal Savings	No repayments

2. (a) and (b)

Account Name: Sales

Date	Details	Dr	Cr	Balance
1 May	Balance		12,250	12,250 cr
2 May	M Prescott		4,000	16,250 cr

Account Name: Purchases

Date	Details	Dr	Cr	Balance
1 May	Balance	3,560		3,560 dr

Account Name: Bank

Date	Details	Dr	Cr	Balance
1 May	Balance	6,220		6,220 dr
7 May	M Prescott	500		6,720 dr

Account Name: Machinery

Date	Details	Dr	Cr	Balance
1 May	Balance	25,600		25,600 dr
7 May	M Prescott	2,000		27,600 dr

Account Name: VAT

Date	Details	Dr	Cr	Balance
2 May	M Prescott		700	700 cr
4 May	M Prescott	35		665 cr

Account Name: M Prescott

Date	Details	Dr	Cr	Balance
2 May	Sales & VAT	4,700		4,700 dr
4 May	Sales Returns & VAT		235	4,465 dr
7 May	Bank		500	3,965 dr
7 May	Machinery		2,000	1,965 dr
7 May	Bad Debts		1,965	0

Account Name: Sales Returns

Date	Details	Dr	Cr	Balance
4 May	M Prescott	200		200 dr

Account Name: Bad Debts

Date	Details	Dr	Cr	Balance
7 May	M Prescott	1,965		1,965 dr

(c) **Explanation:**
Create a Provision for Bad Debts

Effects:
P & L Account
Any one from:
- The amount is entered as an Expense/Income
- This will reduce/increase the Net Profit
- It reduces the profits available for distribution

Balance Sheet
Any one from:
- The PBD is deducted from Debtors
- This will reduce Current Assets/Working Capital/Balance Sheet total
- It gives a more realistic Debtors figure

(d) **Name:**
Suspense Account
And any three from:
- When the errors cannot be found
- This allows the preparation of the final accounts to go ahead
- The difference on the Trial Balance is entered in the Suspense account
- It is recorded in the Balance Sheet; a Dr is a current asset; a Cr is a current liability
- Errors are corrected in the Suspense account
- When all errors are found the Suspense account will have a zero balance

(e) **Explanation:**
Depreciation is the writing down/loss/reduction in the value of fixed assets.
And any two from:
Reasons for allowing for depreciation include:
- Causes of depreciation – wear and tear etc
- Gives a more realistic profit figure for the period
- Fixed Assets are shown at a more realistic value/Book Value
- It spreads the cost over the lifetime of the fixed asset
- Balance Sheet shown at a more realistic value/Book Value

3. (a) **GARDENING DIRECT PLC**
CASH BUDGET FOR JULY & AUGUST 2010

	July	August
Opening Bank/Cash Balance	2,500	11,850
ADD RECEIPTS		
Sales: Cash	5,000	5,000
Credit	32,250	37,000
	39,750	53,850
LESS PAYMENTS		
Purchases	20,000	24,300
Rent	200	200
Insurance	100	100
Wages	1,500	1,500
Electricity	100	100
Interim Preference Dividend	3,000	0
Interim Ordinary Dividend	0	5,000
Delivery Van	3,000	0
	27,900	31,200
Closing Bank/Cash Balance	£11,850	£22,650

(b) *Any two from:*
Benefits of preparing a Cash Budget include:
- Can predict future cash surpluses
- Can arrange payment of debts/purchase of assets
- Can predict future cash shortages and arrange overdrafts/loans
- You know your opening/closing balances
- You can plan for the future
- Can be used to support applications for loans
- Can be used to show prospective investors
- Monitor spending

(c) *Any three from:*
Differences include:
- Preference shares receive a fixed dividend. Ordinary share dividend varies.
- Preference share dividends are paid first before Ordinary share dividends.
- In event of bankruptcy Preference shares are refunded first before Ordinary shares.
- Ordinary shares carry voting rights. Preference usually do not.
- Preference shares are less risky than Ordinary shares.

(d) *Any one from:*
Bank Loan
- Money can be paid back over a period of time

Hire Purchase
- Money paid out over a period of time

Lease
- Not responsible for repairs/maintenance

Grant
- Does not have to be paid back

Buy on Credit
- Pay over a period of time/at a later date

4. (a) (i) **BANK ACCOUNT**

DATE	DETAILS	DR	CR	BAL
31/05/10	Balance	352·40		352·40 dr
	SO – Rent		84·50	267·90 dr
	Correction of Error – Cash		180·00	87·90 dr
	Bank Charges		25·00	62·90 dr
	BGC – Donations	750·00		812·90 dr

(ii)
BANK RECONCILIATION STATEMENT AS AT 31/05/10

Corrected Bank Account Balance		812·90
ADD: Surfequip plc	150·00	
Speed Boatbuilders	2,500·00	2,650·00
		3,462·90
LESS: Subscriptions		500·00
Bank Statement Balance		£2,962·90

or

Bank Statement Balance		2,962·90
LESS: Surfequip plc	150·00	
Speed Boatbuilders	2,500·00	2,650·00
		312·90
ADD: Subscriptions		500·00
Corrected Bank Account Balance		£812·90

(b) Direct Debit
And any one from:
- the person being paid instructs the bank of the amount and time of payment
- the amount can vary each time
- the date of payment can vary each time

or

BGC/BACS
And any one from:
- The person paying the money inform the bank by completing a BGC form or completing the form online
- the amount can vary each time
- the date of payment can vary each time

(c) An Honorarium is a gift given to a club official in recognition of work done for the club by them. It is not a wage and is not based on hours worked but reflects the fact that the work was voluntary.

(d) *Any two from:*
- ◆ Refreshments/Shop/Bar Trading A/c
  And any one from:
  - to show profit/loss made on bar
  - to indicate how bar expenses may be controlled
  - to show cost of bar supplies

- ◆ Supplementary Income Statements
  - can show profit/loss made by fundraising events

- ◆ Income & Expenditure A/c
  And any one from:
  - to show Surplus/Deficit for the year as opposed to cash position
  - to indicate how profitability may be improved

- ◆ Balance Sheet
  And any one from:
  - to show what the club is worth
  - to show assets owned by club
  - to show liabilities of the club

5. (a) (i) **NIVEN & BROWN P&L APPROPRIATION ACCOUNT FOR YEAR ENDED 31/03/10**

	£	£	£
NET PROFIT			23,500
LESS APPROPRIATIONS:			
Salary – Brown		3,500	
INTEREST ON CAPITAL:			
Niven	9,000		
Brown	3,000	12,000	15,500
RESIDUAL PROFIT			8,000
SHARE OF PROFITS:			
Niven		6,000	
Brown		2,000	8,000
			0

(ii)

CURRENT A/C – Niven		DR	CR	BAL
01/04/2009	Balance	4,500		4,500 dr
31/03/2010	Interest on Capital		9,000	4,500 cr
	Share of Profit		6,000	10,500 cr
	Drawings	2,500		8,000 cr

CURRENT A/C – Brown		DR	CR	BAL
01/04/2009	Balance		1,900	1,900 cr
31/03/2010	Interest on Capital		3,000	4,900 cr
	Share of Profit		2,000	6,900 cr
	Drawings	3,500		10,400 cr

(b) Benefits of operating as a Partnership rather than a Sole Trader include:
Any two from:
- More Capital, expertise, ideas, borrowing power
- Help with decision making
- Easier to get time off
- Losses, workload, responsibility, debts are shared

Costs of operating as a Partnership rather than a Sole Trader include:
Any two from:
- Loss of control/no longer own boss
- Have to share profit
- Need to consult
- Disagreements
- Possibility of partner ruining business

(c) Reasons Brown is entitled to a Partnership Salary include:
Any one from:
- Puts in more hours/work
- Has extra skill/expertise
- Takes more responsibility
- Performs special duties (key holder)
- Niven is a sleeping partner

6. (a) NP% = NP/Sales × 100

$$\frac{3,000}{120,000} \times 100 = 2.5\%$$

ROST = COS*/AV ST**

$$\frac{102,000}{6,000} = 17 \text{ times}$$

*COS = Sales – GP
120,000 – 18,000
or
*COS = (OP ST + PURCH) – CL ST
(6,500 + 101,000) – 5,500

**Av St = (Op St + Cl St)/2
(6,500 + 5,500)/2

(b) Reasons for difference between "average firm" and Brian's results include:
Any one from:
NP% – Brian has higher expenses
– Brian has a lower Gross Profit
– Brian has a lower selling price
– Brian has lower "Other Incomes"

Any one from:
ROST – Brian has a lower selling price
– Brian carries less stock
– Brian has carried out/spent more on advertising
– Brian has a better buying policy
– Brian makes more/quicker sales

(c) *Any two from:*

GP% OR GP/SALES × 100
- To see the percentage of sales that is turned into Gross Profit

EXPENSES% OR EXPENSES/SALES × 100
- To see how much of income from sales is taken up by expenses

MARK UP% OR GP/COS × 100
- To see the percentage of profit that is added on to cost price

WORKING CAPITAL/CURRENT (RATIO) OR CA : CL
- To see the firm's ability to meet short term debts and pay day-to-day running costs

ACID TEST RATIO OR (CA-ST) : CL
- As above but stock removed to use only "liquid" current assets

ROCE OR NP/CAP AT START × 100
- To see how much the owner(s) get back from their investment

GENERAL REASONS
Any one from:
- To see how well the business is doing
- To compare with other companies
- To compare with industry average
- To compare with previous years
- To highlight areas of concern
- To aid planning

ACCOUNTING & FINANCE GENERAL 2011

1. (a)

Quantity	Description	Unit Price £	Cost £
10	Pasta Bowls	8.00	80.00
4	Large Platters	10.00	40.00
			120.00
	Less 5% Trade Discount		6.00
	Net Goods Value		114.00
	Add VAT @ (17·5%)		19.95
	Total		**£133.95**

(b)
- Purchases
- VAT
- Sam Stenhouse

(c)
- In the same trade
- To attract customers
- To encourage repeat custom
- To encourage bulk buying
- To sell more

(d) (i)
- Statement (of Account)

(ii)
- It gives a record of the month's transactions
- It shows the closing balance **or** it shows how much is still owed
- It shows when payment is due
- It shows purchases and returns **or** invoices and credit notes **or** payments and discounts

(e)
- No need for cash
- Pay at a later date
- Pay in instalments
- Time to sell goods before paying
- Improves cash flow

2. (a) (i) & (ii)

Account Name:	Castle Contractors			Number 1		
Date	Details	Dr		Cr		Balance
		£	p	£	p	£	p
1/2/11	Balance	350	00			350	00
5/2/11	Sales and VAT	524	94			874	94
14/2/11	Sales Returns and VAT			83	97	790	97
18/2/11	Bank			327	50	463	47
18/2/11	Discount Allowed			22	50	440	97

Account Name: Sales						Number 2	
Date	Details	Dr		Cr		Balance	
		£	p	£	p	£	p
5/2/11	Castle Contractors			450	00	450	00

Account Name: VAT						Number 3	
Date	Details	Dr		Cr		Balance	
		£	p	£	p	£	p
5/2/11	Castle Contractors			74	94	74	94
14/2/11	Castle Contractors	11	97			62	97

Account Name: Sales Returns						Number 4	
Date	Details	Dr		Cr		Balance	
		£	p	£	p	£	p
14/2/11	Castle Contractors	72	00			72	00

Account Name: Bank						Number 5	
Date	Details	Dr		Cr		Balance	
		£	p	£	p	£	p
18/2/11	Castle Contractors	327	50			327	50

Account Name: Discount Allowed						Number 6	
Date	Details	Dr		Cr		Balance	
		£	p	£	p	£	p
18/2/11	Castle Contractors	22	50			22	50

(b) (i) • One DR entry and one CR entry
- Corresponding entries on DR and CR
- Example of a transaction
- Each transaction is entered twice in the ledger accounts

(ii) • Trial Balance

(iii) • Trading A/c/Profit and Loss A/c
- Balance Sheet

(c) (i) • Increased capital
- Easier to take time off/holidays
- Shared workload/shared decision-making/shared losses
- Increased expertise
- Easier to borrow
- Shared debt in event of bankruptcy

(ii) • Unlimited liability
- Shared profits
- Disagreements
- Slower decision-making
- Loss of control
- Responsible for partners actions
- Partnership ceases if partner leaves/dies/retires

3. (a) **CASH BUDGET FOR JULY AND AUGUST 2011**

	July £	August £
OPENING BALANCE	4,000	3,350
Receipts		
Credit Sales	1,800	2,400
Cash Sales	1,200	1,500
	7,000	7,250
Payments		
Purchases	1,300	1,250
Rent	1,200	1,200
Wages	750	750
Advertising	400	400
ICT Equipment	0	1,750
	3,650	5,350
CLOSING BALANCE	3,350	1,900

(b)
Description	Source of Finance
Borrowing specifically for the purchase of property	*Mortgage*
Long-term loans which must be repaid in full at an agreed date	*Debentures*
Short-term borrowing to ease cash flow	*Overdraft*

(c) (i) Dividend
- **Share of profits paid to shareholders**
- **Return on investment**

(ii) Wages Accrued
- **Wages due for the current period**
- **Wages not yet been paid**
- **Liability in the Balance Sheet**

(d) • Shareholders loss is limited to their investment
- Shareholders cannot lose their personal possessions
- Shareholders are not personally liable for the debts of the business

4. (a)

BANK ACCOUNT

Date	Details	Dr	Cr	Balance
		£	£	£
30 April	Balance	345.00		345.00
30 April	DD – Topdeal Insurance		35.00	310.00
30 April	BGC – Sponsorship	44.50		354.50
30 April	Bank Charges		14.50	340.00

(b) **Bank Reconciliation Statement of Larkside Drama Club as at 30 April 2011**

Balance as per (Bank) Statement		315.00
ADD Amounts not Credited		
Donation		120.00
		435.00
LESS Unpresented Cheques		
Jack Joinery Ltd	75.00	
Advertising	20.00	95.00
Balance as per (updated) Bank Account		340.00

or

Balance as per (updated) Bank Account		340.00
ADD Unpresented Cheques		
Jack Joinery Ltd	75.00	
Advertising	20.00	95.00
		435.00
LESS Amounts not Credited		
Donation		120.00
Balance as per (Bank) Statement		315.00

(c)
- For safe keeping of money/valuables
- For providing services
- Cost of overdraft/Overdraft interest
- To make a profit
- Penalty for late payment

(d)
- Treasurer

(e) **Deficit** –
- Expenditure greater than income;
- Opposite of surplus;
- Loss in Income/Exp A/c

AGM – Annual General Meeting; a meeting that all members can attend; office bearers are elected; financial statements are presented

Honorarium – Payment/gift to Secretary/Treasurer/Club Official for voluntary work done for club for professional services – not a wage

5. (a) (i) **Rate of Stock Turnover**

$$\text{Average stock} = \frac{\text{stock at start + stock at end}}{2}$$

$$\frac{15,000 + 9,000}{2} = \frac{24,000}{2} = £12,000$$

$$\frac{\text{Cost of goods sold}}{\text{average stock}} = \frac{72,000}{12,000} = 6 \text{ times}$$

(ii) **Gross Profit Percentage**

$$\frac{£48,000}{£120,00} \times \frac{100}{1} = 40\%$$

(iii) **Net Profit Percentage**

$$\frac{£15,000}{£120,00} \times \frac{100}{1} = 12.5\%$$

(b)
- Cost of transporting purchases
- Cost of transport
- Cost of getting your stock
- Delivery costs/Postage

(c)
- Changed or improved purchasing policy
- Cheaper supplier
- Advertising/Special Offers
- Holding less stock
- Selling more stock
- Selling slow moving items/Having a sale
- Increased Sales
- Decrease in selling price

(d)
- Working Capital (Current) Ratio
- Return on Capital Invested/Employed
- Mark up
- Expenses Ratio
- Acid Test Ratio
- Example of an Expense to Sales ratio

(e)
- NP will increase the capital
- NP is added to capital

6. (a) **Appropriation Account of Benito and Moreno for year ended 30 April 2011**

		£	£
Net Profit			42,000
Less: Salaries –	Benito	8,000	
	Moreno	10,000	18,000
(Residual Profit)			24,000
Share of Profit –	Benito	16,000	
	Moreno	8,000	24,000

(b)

Moreno – Current Account				
Date	Details	Dr	Cr	Balance
		£	£	£
30 April	Balance		1,000	1,000
	Salary		10,000	11,000
	Drawings	5,000		6,000
	Share of Profits		8,000	14,000

(c) (i)
- Purchase of fixed assets
- Spending on items which will be used in the business over a long period of time
- Will appear in Balance Sheet

(ii)
- Purchase of premises/equipment/vehicles
- Repayment of a loan

(iii)
- Spending on items which will be used up in current year
- Day-to-day running costs
- Expenses in P & L A/c

(iv)
- Rent/wages/insurance/advertising/etc
- Purchases/Stock/General or Misc expenses

(d) • **Depreciation** – reduction in value of a <u>fixed</u> asset due to wear/tear/Expense in P & L A/c/obsolescence/damage/age.

• **Bad Debts** – Debtors who have become bankrupt; debts which cannot be paid; debtor who cannot pay written off as an expense in P and L Account.

• **Creditor** – Someone the business owes money to; a current liability; someone the business has bought goods on credit from; a liability in the Balance Sheet.

ACCOUNTING & FINANCE CREDIT 2011

1. (a)

Date	Details	Dr	Cr	Balance
		£	£	£
01/03/11	Balance	524·81		524·81 dr
07/03/11	Sales	818·70		1,343·51 dr
10/03/11	Bank		502·31	841·20 dr
10/03/11	Discount		22·50	818·70 dr
15/03/11	Returns		265·00	553·70 dr

07/03/11	Sales		780·00
	LESS Trade Discount (10%)		78·00
	NGV		702·00
	ADD VAT*		116·70
	TOTAL		£818·70
*VAT	NGV		702·00
	LESS Cash Discount (5%)		35·10
			666·90
	VAT (17·5%)		£116·70

(b) To encourage their customers to pay:
Any one from:
• within the time mentioned in the "terms"/within the month
• promptly
• to help their cash flow.

(c) **Credit Note**
• Used to record a return of goods
• Previously bought on credit
• States reason for return
• Reduces amount originally owed
• Used to record entries in the ledger
• Shows details of goods returned

(d) Any two from:

ADVANTAGES	DISADVANTAGES
More capital (available from shares)	No longer in control of business
More expertise (from BOD)	Profits shared between people/shareholders
More sources of finance (debentures)	Legal requirements have to be met/must publish accounts/must hold AGM
Limited liability	May not receive any dividends
Easier to borrow (due to size)	Shares may lose value
More purchasing power	Expensive to set up

2. (*a*) & (*b*)

CASH ACCOUNT

01/03/11	Balance	455·00		455·00 dr
06/03/11	Sales & VAT	235·00		690·00 dr
08/03/11	Equipment & VAT	35·25		725·25 dr
10/03/11	Bank		675·25	50·00 dr

BANK ACCOUNT

01/03/11	Balance		220·00	220·00 cr
02/03/11	Equipment & VAT		141·00	361·00 cr
10/03/11	Cash	675·25		314·25 dr

EQUIPMENT ACCOUNT

01/03/11	Balance	2,100·00		2,100·00 dr
02/03/11	Bank	120·00		2,220·00 dr
04/03/11	Drawings		30·00	2,190·00 dr
08/03/11	Cash		30·00	2,160·00 dr

VAT ACCOUNT

02/03/11	Bank	21·00		21·00 dr
04/03/11	Drawings		5·25	15·75 dr
06/03/11	Cash		35·00	19·25 cr
08/03/11	Cash		5·25	24·50 cr

DRAWINGS ACCOUNT

04/03/11	Equipment & VAT	35·25		35·25 dr

SALES ACCOUNT

06/03/11	Cash		200·00	200·00 cr

(*c*) **Advantages of operating on a credit basis include:**
Any two from:
- wider range of customers – increased sales
- increased customer loyalty
- larger orders more likely.

Disadvantages of operating on a credit basis include:
Any two from:
- (likelihood of) bad debts/cost of credit checks
- liquidity/cashflow problems
- cost of borrowing
- increased accounting procedures.

(*d*) *Any two from:*
- **Refreshments/Shop/Bar Trading A/c**
  to show profit/loss made on bar
  to indicate how bar expenses may be controlled
  to show cost of bar supplies.
- **Income Statements**
  can show profit/loss made by events/activities.
- **An Income & Expenditure A/c**
  to show <u>revenue</u> income and expenditure
  to show Surplus/Deficit for the year (as opposed to cash position)
  to indicate how profitability may be improved.
- **Balance Sheet**
  to show what the club is worth/accumulated fund
  to show assets owned by club
  to show liabilities of the club.

- **Cash Budget**
  can predict future cash surpluses
  arrange payment of debts
  arrange purchase of assets
  can predict future cash shortages
  arrange overdrafts
  arrange loans
  you know your opening/closing balances
  you can plan for the future
  can be used to support applications for loans/show prospective investors.

3. (*a*) Sales/qty = SP £15,000/30,000
   = £0·50

Cost of Sales/qty = VC £9,000/30,000
   = £0·30

Total Exp = FC £2,000 + £200 + £1,800
   = £4,000

SP – VC = Unit Contribution £0·50 - £0·30
   = £0·20

FC/Unit Contribution = BEP £4,000/£0·20
   = 20,000 hamburgers

(*b*) New FC/Unit Contribution = 4,200/£0·20
New BEP = 21,000 hamburgers

(*c*) Required Profit + FC = Required Contribution
(£5000) (£4200) = (£9200)

Required Contribution/Unit Contribution per hamburger = No of hamburgers

£9,200/£0·20 = 46,000 hamburgers

(*d*) (i) It will decrease the BEP as the contribution per unit will be a higher figure being divided into the same (fixed) costs to get BEP, contribution will change

(ii) It will decrease the BEP as the contribution per unit will again be a higher figure being divided into the same fixed costs, contribution will change

(*e*) (i) more shares
debentures

(ii) **SHARES**
Any one from:
Advantages
- Do not have to be paid back
- No interest repayments required
- Dividend can be decided by BOD
- Can get a large sum of money

Any one from:
Disadvantages
- May have to pay extra dividends
- Ownership & control are diluted
- Investors may not be interested
- Cost of issue

DEBENTURES
Any one from:
Advantages
- Only interest is paid until repayment date
- Final payment in future giving time to save/organise
- No loss/dilution of ownership/control
- Long term loan
- Can get a large sum of money

Any one from:
Disadvantages
- Interest has to be paid
- Final repayment has to be made in lump sum
- Profits reduced due to interest
- Extra liability

4. (*a*) **FLIES ARE US**
TRADING, PROFIT & LOSS ACCOUNT
FOR YEAR ENDED 30 APRIL 2011

	£	£	£
Sales			73,250
LESS: COST OF SALES			
Opening Stock		4,600	
ADD: Purchases	24,650		
ADD: Carriage Inwards	175		
	24,825		
LESS: Returns Outwards	900	23,925	
		28,525	
LESS: Closing Stock		5,000	23,525
GROSS PROFIT			49,725
ADD: OTHER INCOME			
Rent Received			1,200
			50,925
LESS: EXPENSES			
Wages (20,000+1,000)		21,000	
Carriage Outwards		350	
Electricity (1,540-90)		1,450	
Bad Debts		150	
Increase in PBD (3,000*10%)-200		100	
Depreciation (of Van) (10,000*15%)		1,500	
Loan Interest		200	24,750
NET PROFIT			26,175

(*b*) (i) • Carriage is the cost of transporting goods.
- Outwards means the goods are going out of our business. Inwards means the goods are coming into our business.
- Carriage Outwards is the cost of transporting sales from our business to our customers. It is recorded as an expense in the P & L A/c.
- Carriage Inwards is the cost of transporting purchases from our suppliers to our business. It is added to Purchases in the Trading A/c.

(ii) • A debtor is someone we have sold goods on credit to and they therefore owe us money. They are shown in the Balance Sheet as a Current Asset.
- A creditor is someone we have purchased goods on credit from and we therefore owe them money. They are shown in the Balance Sheet as a Current Liability.

(iii) • Bad Debts occur when debtors fail to pay the amount owed. It is an expense in the P&L Account. It does not affect the Debtors total as the account has already been closed.
- The Provision for Bad Debts is an attempt to anticipate future Bad Debts.
Only the difference from one year to another is shown in the P&L Account.
An increase is an Expense, a decrease is Other Income. It is deducted from Debtors in the Balance Sheet to give a more realistic Debtors figure.

5. (*a*) & (*b*)

DATE	DETAILS	DR	CR	BAL
SUSPENSE ACCOUNT				
1 March	Difference on TB	892·00		892·00 dr
	Sales Returns		500·00	392·00 dr
	Drawings – B Boyle		466·00	74·00 cr
	Cash		216·00	299·00 cr
	Purchases	290·00		0

(*c*) • Error of principle
- Error of commission

(*d*) *Any two from:*
- Error of Omission. When no entries have been made for a transaction either in dr or cr eg an invoice falling down the back of the filing cabinet and being forgotten about.
- Error of Original Entry. When the wrong figure is used in all entries for a transaction eg payment of an expense of £624 is recorded in the expense and money accounts as £642.
- Compensating Errors. When one or more errors cancel each other out eg a wrong dr of £50 is cancelled out by wrong cr entries of £23 and £27.
- Complete Reversal. When the entries for a transaction are completely reversed ie the account that should have been dr is cr whilst the account that should have been cr is dr eg payment of an expense is cr to expense account and dr to money account.

(*e*) The above errors would not affect the balancing of the Trial Balance as in all cases the Debit entries made are equal to the Credit entries made.
The double entry has been completed.

6. (*a*)

RATIO	PEDLARS	CYCLING WORLD
WORKING CAPITAL/ CURRENT RATIO = CA : CL	11000: 7750 1.42 : 1	4500 : 1500 3 : 1
RETURN ON CAPITAL EMPLOYED (INVESTED) NP/CAP AT BEGINNING * 100	35000/85000 * 100 41.18%	2500/30000 * 100 83.33%

(*b*) Gross Profit % (1) = GP/Sales x 100
Any one from:
- Shows % profit being made from buying/selling stock
- Can show if Selling Price needs to be increased
- Shows how well business is doing
- Can be compared to: previous years
   other businesses
   industry average

Rate of Stock Turnover = Cost of Sales/Av St
Any one from:
- Shows how quickly stock is being sold
- Can avoid build up of stock
- Lets you know how quickly to re-order

Net Profit % (1) = NP/Sales x 100
Any one from:
- Shows how profitable the company is after expenses have been deducted
- Can indicate changes in GP%

(c) A Sole Trader
Any one from:
- The business has only one person injecting Capital
- The Net Profit is going in full to the owner
- The Drawings are being taken from the owner's capital

(d) Closing Capital may be less than Opening Capital because:
Any two from:
- the owner has taken TOO much out in Drawings
- more drawings than NP
- the business made a Net Loss
- the owner has withdrawn some of their capital.

(e) Banking Services to pay an electricity bill could be:
Any two from:
- Direct Debit
- Standing Order
- BGC

Most appropriate method is Direct Debit as:
Any one from:
- the amount can vary
- the recipient informs bank of amount due
- the date can vary

Hey! I've done it

BrightRED
PUBLISHING

© 2011 SQA/Bright Red Publishing Ltd, All Rights Reserved
Published by Bright Red Publishing Ltd, 6 Stafford Street, Edinburgh, EH3 7AU
Tel: 0131 220 5804, Fax: 0131 220 6710, enquiries: sales@brightredpublishing.co.uk,
www.brightredpublishing.co.uk

Official SQA answers to 978-1-84948-156-4
2007-2011